**Pembrokeshire College,
Learning Resource Centre,
Haverfordwest SA61 1SZ
Telephone: 01437 – 765247**

Return on or before the ~~~~ below.

P 03466

T~~~~AME

BADMINTON

Peter Roper

County Coach,
Badminton Association of England

The Cro

D0260078

First published in 1985 by
The Crowood Press Ltd
Ramsbury, Marlborough
Wiltshire SN8 2HR

Revised edition 1995
This impression 1999

© The Crowood Press Ltd 1985 and 1995

All rights reserved. No part of this publication may be reproduced or transmitted in any form or by any means, electronic or mechanical, including photocopy, recording, or any information storage and retrieval system, without permission in writing from the publishers.

British Library Cataloguing-in-Publication Data

A catalogue record for this book is available
from the British Library

ISBN 1 85223 887 9

Acknowledgements

Action photographs by Peter Richardson
Demonstration photographs by Phil Reeson
Line illustrations by Annette Findlay

Series Adviser C.E. Bond MEd, AdvDipPE, DLC (Hons),
Head of PE, Carnegie School of Physical Education and Human
Movement Studies

Printed in Great Britain by
The Bath Press

Contents

Peter Roper is a county coach, assessor, verifier and tutor for the Badminton Association of England, and has been involved in playing and coaching badminton for over thirty-five years.

He has held a number of coaching and administrative posts, but more recently has concentrated his activities on specialised coaching and training for small groups of international and county players.

In this book Peter Roper offers the reader a wealth of information on how to play and improve at badminton.

As a keen student and analyst of the game he has acquired a comprehensive knowledge of the game, which is increased by his experience in coaching players from beginner to international standard. To this he adds his extensive experience in educating and training coaches for the Badminton Association of England.

In writing this book, Peter has drawn on his knowledge to share with readers his ideas, advice and practical methods for learning the basic skills of the game, and for practising and playing singles and level mixed doubles.

It is a book well worth reading if you are starting to play badminton or if you simply want to become a better player.

Jake Downey
Director of Coaching, Badminton Association of England

Peter Roper has been playing and coaching badminton for many years, holding several coaching and administrative appointments, but more recently concentrating on specialised coaching and training of small groups of international and county players.

He is an authority of long standing and great experience, especially on coaching. His book is well researched and full of valuable information for those who are keen to make progress in the sport.

W.G.P. Birtwistle
President, The Badminton Association of England

Introduction

Badminton, a game played with rackets and shuttlecocks, takes its name from the Duke of Beaufort's seat in Gloucestershire, England. It was first played in England in 1873, but before that time was played in India by officers of the British Army.

The Badminton Association of England was founded in 1893, the first All-England Championships, long recognised as the unofficial world championships, being held in 1899. The first international match, between England and Ireland, was played in 1903.

From its small and rather select beginnings, the game has grown to become one of the most popular participant sports in Great Britain, now enjoyed by millions of players at all levels of ability. There are many thousands of clubs affiliated to the national bodies of England, Scotland, Wales and Northern Ireland and probably far more unaffiliated. With the advent of multi-purpose sports centres the game is now, more than ever before, available to players wishing to enjoy it.

The International Badminton Federation was founded in 1934, its nine founder members including England, Ireland, Scotland and Wales. In 1994 the Federation boasted a membership of 134 nations, an indication of the world-wide appeal of the game as is its inclusion in the Olympic Games. There are also World Championships for both individuals and national mixed teams as well as the Thomas and Uber Cups, which are world championships for men's and ladies' teams respectively. While European players have enjoyed success in the World Championships, and two English ladies have taken titles in the past, the bulk of Olympic, World Individual and Team, and Thomas and Uber Cup titles have been shared between Malaya, China, Indonesia and South Korea.

In England the game is played at all levels and ages ranging from school children (there is a well-organised English Schools Badminton Association) through to Fifty Plus groups. Competitions abound for both children and adults, from local leagues to international matches via the inter-county championships, and both restricted and Open county tournaments. International players now have an itinerary of ranking tournaments which requires them to travel world-wide throughout the year. The demands of training, travel and competition are now such that most of these players devote their entire time to the game.

EQUIPMENT

For the beginner a large number of sports centres now offer the opportunity for playing the game without having to join a club. Most sports centres regularly hold courses of instruction and all county associations provide courses for players wishing to advance their ability.

Initially complete beginners will require very little equipment as most of the sports centres have arrangements for hiring rackets, possibly the most expensive item you will need. Should they already be playing a racket sport, most of their clothing, with the possible exception of footwear, will be suitable for badminton.

Clothing

If you intend to play the game at all seriously you should be aware that most competition organisers will require clothing to be predominantly white. Many badminton equipment manufacturers specialise in providing clothing to meet this requirement. Your local sports retailer will be able to offer an extremely wide choice. Men will require shirt, shorts and socks; ladies, skirt or shorts, shirts and socks. Clothing should be light, not too loose-fitting and made of a sweat-absorbent material. The very keen player may require a number of changes as wet clothing is not only uncomfortable, it can be positively unsocial! Socks should be knitted in all, or mostly, wool, as this is most comfortable for the feet. Synthetic materials can be abrasive with devastating effects on the feet! In addition it is recommended that you have a track-suit to serve a number of purposes: it will assist warm-up, maintain body temperature between games and prevent too rapid warm-down.

Footwear

The provision of suitable shoes for sporting activities is now very specialised and your sports dealer should be able to cater for your specific requirements. Most sports centres have vinyl-covered floors and will not permit black-soled shoes to be worn. Your shoes, in addition to being able to withstand punishment, can also impart considerable damage to your feet if wrongly sized. If your precise fit is not available it is recommended that shoes one half size too large and an additional pair of socks be worn. Ensure you have 'broken-in' the shoes before strenuous play by wearing them about the house for a few days after purchase. Keen players will require more than one pair of shoes, each with different sole tread patterns, to cope with the different playing surfaces encountered from one hall to another.

Rackets

The choice varies from the extremely cheap (usually supplied in 'garden badminton' sets) to the very expensive. Very few rackets, if any, are now produced in the original, totally laminated wood design. Over the past few years technology has greatly improved so rackets are all now of light weight. Types available vary from all steel, at the cheap end of the price range, to all-carbon construction, at the very expensive end. The complete beginner may prefer to hire a racket from the sports centre before committing to a purchase. When purchasing you will find the sports retailer's stock will be extensive and possibly confusing. Your first consideration will be the amount of money you are prepared to spend. After that consider the weight, balance and 'feel' of the racket. The lighter a racket the faster you should be able to move it – an important factor. Balance should not be too biased towards either head or handle. Check this by balancing the racket on a finger about half-way between both ends. Preferably select a racket which is slightly 'head-heavy'. There are usually two grip diam-eters available and the advice here is that while modern racket grips can be built up, with towelling or similar wrapping, it is impossible to reduce the size. Grip diameter is extremely important. Too large and gripping can restrict hand manipulation by use of the forearm muscles (wrist action) in shot making; too small may require a clenched fist hitting action with, again, adverse effects on shot making. Almost universally rackets are supplied with synthetic stringing which allows the very tight tensions favoured by most players, but old-fashioned gut, allowing slightly more 'feel', is also available. Most rackets are supplied with a head cover providing protection to frame and stringing when the racket is not is use.

Sports Bag

You should always shower immediately after strenuous exercise and change into dry clothing. A sports bag is, therefore, an item which you should have from the outset. Ensure that it is of adequate size to take clothing, shoes, towel, etc. It should totally enclose your racket(s) and have a separate compartment for damp clothing and towel.

Shuttlecocks

Two choices are available, either the traditional feather or its modern counterpart, the synthetic. Feather shuttlecocks are universally recognised as the best. Produced from goose feathers (only a few

from each wing – the geese suffer no harm) they have a superior flight pattern and 'feel' off the racket to any of their competitors but they are fragile and expensive. Because of their light weight most have small weights in the cork base to provide different 'weights' and therefore speeds. This is very important as all halls have individual conditions of air density and humidity, which considerably affect the length of flight of the shuttlecocks. There are six 'speeds' commonly used in this country ranging from 77 to 82. The highest numbers are heaviest and travel furthest. Synthetic shuttlecocks were introduced to counter the constantly increasing cost of feathers. Technology has greatly improved their construction so that, in many respects, they are very comparable to their feather counterparts. Most are now available with kid-covered cork bases and in varying speeds other than slow, medium or fast. The most expensive equate in price to the cheapest feathers but have substantial advantages in durability.

Joining a Club

As your ability increases you should consider joining a club. This will provide more opportunities for improvement, introduce you to other enthusiasts and allow entry in club team matches and other competitions as your ability improves. Enquiries regarding clubs in your area should be directed to your county association secretary whose address and telephone number will be available from your national association (*see* Useful Addresses).

1
Basic Stroke Making

INTRODUCTION

Badminton is predominantly a 'perceptual skill' requiring an ability to anticipate without being anticipated, to see and react to each cue in the game situation early and effectively. There is a need for the player to counter an opponent's move effectively in order to survive but, also, if he is more often to win than lose, to ensure that those counters are unique, or not often encountered within the experience of his opponents.

As badminton is a complex sporting activity the learning of the many skills which make up the best players will require a great deal of time.They will need:

1. A high level of fitness.
2. An ability to play all of the shots within the game effectively, with total consistency and accuracy, imaginatively and with great creativity.
3. To develop both the desire to win and a dogged determination not to be defeated.

All players were at one time beginners. As such they soon learnt that striking a shuttle is only one of the elements of the game. In order to compete within a game situation, they also had to learn:

1. To make judgements regarding the different paces, trajectories and angles of the shuttle when in flight.

2. To react and respond very quickly to the various stimuli so that they reached the shuttle before it struck the floor and in time to play an effective reply.
3. To present the body in the right place and the correct striking attitude immediately prior to hitting the shuttle in order maximise shot making.
4. To strike the shuttle in a manner that ensured maximum results without compromising recovery from the shot played and movement to the next.
5. To move about the court effectively and above all efficiently.

All these elements are essential to becoming a competent badminton player and whilst they can and, in the initial learning stages, must be considered in isolation, they should be practised in total as soon as opportunity and ability allow. Initially beginners must be occupied in learning the basic skills to the exclusion of game play. Only when there is an improvement in these skills and a greater knowledge of the game should formal game play be introduced.

BASIC STROKE MAKING

There are six stroke (prepare – travel – hit – recover) actions to consider, namely, underarm, shoulder high and overhead, played from the fore, mid and back court areas respectively, with either forehand or backhand actions. From these six strokes are played a number of shots which allow us to hit shuttles to the opponent's fore, mid or back courts. All the strokes have a number of common elements, distinct differences between forehand and backhand strokes and then smaller variations for each of the shots.

Forehand Strokes and Shots – these, for the right-handed player, are those shots played in front of, or to the right of, the body. They are played below the shoulder, at shoulder level or above the shoulder.

Backhand Strokes and Shots – again for the right-handed player, these are those shots played on the left-hand side of the body whether below, at or above shoulder level.

The Grips

Here we are considering the manner in which to hold the racket in order to best utilise the other elements of shot making. The manner in which we hold the racket must be the *result of* not the *reason for* the other elements. One without the others will compromise the quality of shot produced, movement about court, and so on. The term 'grip' is a misnomer as we must hold the racket neither too tightly or loosely when striking the shuttle. Gripping the racket too tightly not only restricts the use of the arm and shoulder muscles but, particularly, our ability to 'cock' and 'uncock' hand and fingers at the wrist by using the forearm muscles. Conversely, holding the racket too loosely will allow the racket head to turn when striking, thus leading to the shuttle being struck with less force and direction than intended. There are other, slightly modified ways of holding the racket

for serving, receiving and hitting at the net which will be considered later under their specific shot headings. For basic stroke and shot making we have two ways in which we can hold the racket which, as this is the term commonly used, will be called 'grips'.

FOREHAND GRIP
(Fig 1)
The objective is to strike the shuttle with the palm of the hand, first and second fingers slightly extended. This action is to be extended through and into the racket head. Pick up the racket and 'shake hands' with the racket grip, firmly but not tightly, first and second fingers slightly extended, the butt (the enlarged section at the bottom of the racket) just within the span of the hand. Ensure that the face of the racket head is in the same plane as the palm of the hand – remember – palm of hand must become face of racket head. By extending the arm downwards in front of the body you should now see the edge of the racket head – not the stringing – in line with the V formed by the thumb and first finger.

Shadow a number of imaginary shots by swinging the racket down in front of the body, to the side of the body at shoulder height and with the arm fully extended above the head. Is the grip firm but comfortable? Can you comfortably flex wrist and elbow, particularly above the shoulder? At the point of imaginary impact will the shuttle be projected in the intended direction?

BACKHAND GRIP
(Fig 2)
The objective is to strike the shuttle when it is on the left of the body with the knuckles of the back of the hand ('feeling' the impact in

9

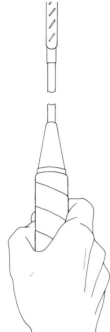

Fig 1 Forehand grip – looking down extended arm to see outer edge of frame of racket head.

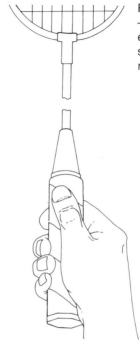

Fig 2 Backhand grip – looking down extended arm to see stringing and frame of racket head.

the tip of the thumb). This action is extended through and into the racket head. Hold the racket with the loose forehand grip described above, turn the racket head slightly to the right and adjust your grip so that you can now press firmly, not too hard, with the touch area of the thumb onto the flat of the racket grip which now presents itself. Extending the arm in front of the body you should now see the stringing surrounded by the frame as you look down the thumb.

Again shadow a number of imaginary shots on the left-hand side of the body ensuring that the grip is firm but comfortable, that you can comfortably flex the wrist and elbow particularly above the shoulder – and that, at the point of imaginary impact, the shuttle will be projected in the intended direction.

Reminder – the above instructions were for right-handed players. If you are left-handed the instructions should be 'handed', i.e. for the right read left and vice versa.

Having established the two basic ways of holding the racket (the grips) let us now consider the other essential basic elements of stroke/shot making. In order to allow the beginner to make the earliest possible progress with some form of practice, first hitting without moving, thereafter a step at a time, these are presented in reverse order.

Follow-after

This is usually described as 'follow-through' but this, in most instances, is a misnomer. The impact effort, particularly when hard, should follow after and along the intended trajectory of the shuttle.

Follow-after is a consideration with all shots to the extent that for some shots it is important *not* to follow after. For others, it is a positive aid to recovery. Importantly, failing to follow after some of the powerful shots may prove injurious to muscles.

In general terms, forehand shots have follow-after, backhand shots have no follow-after other than of hand and, therefore, racket head. In view of the number of variables that can be applied, follow-after is considered specifically under each shot description.

Cocking and Uncocking the Hand
(Fig 3)

In order to induce fast head speed the racket is flexed backwards first away from the shuttle and then forwards to hit it The hand is manipulated around the wrist joint axis by use of the forearm muscles. It is an extremely important part of the hitting technique. Fast, not necessarily very strong, movements of the hand (the cocking and uncocking action) greatly accelerates the speed of racket head prior to hitting the shuttle.

To maximise this action it is essential that the grip is not too tight so that the action truly realises the objective of very quickly 'cocking' then 'uncocking' the hand. The action should not be overly exaggerated, but come as a natural extension of vigorously throwing the racket arm at point of impact.

Later we will consider the deliberate use of wrist action to create slice and changes of direction.

Arm Straightening
(Figs 4–7)

All shots should be played with some degree of arm movement prior to striking the shuttle. This varies between vigorous arm throwing and small movements of the forearm. Initially these movements may be deliberate and exaggerated. Progressively they should become faster-flowing and truncated to impact 'snap' into hitting. The illustrations show examples of 'bent arm' and 'hand cocked' preparation to shuttle striking employed by world renowned players.

Upper Body Movement
(Figs 4–7)

Particularly with shots played above the shoulders, upper body movement is an essential ingredient of good shot making. Additional pace is put into shot making by

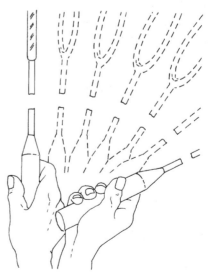

Fig 3   Wrist action – showing rapid movement of racket head created by 'uncocking' and 'cocking' strongly.

11

Fig 4   Lim Xiaoqing of Sweden just about to play an overhead forehand shot. Note body attitude, non-racket hand extension, how racket arm is bent, the forehand grip and how shot is played off the racket foot.

Fig 5   Steve Butler of England, literally at point of impact. Note how the back is to the net, the body is fully extended upwards with hands balanced above feet and the hand uncocked.

Fig 6   Anders Nielsen of England still having a little further to go to reach the underarm forehand shot in the forecourt. By then he will be into a fully extended lunge with hands balanced above feet. The racket still shows no indication of his intentions.

Fig 7   Catrine Bergtsson of Sweden, showing the very dynamic fast forward movement required to reach into the forecourt to play an underarm net shot. Again note the balancing effect of hands above feet.

twisting the upper body, especially the racket shoulder, first away from, then into and through the hitting arc. In addition to improving shot making techniques, upper body movement greatly assists movement to and from that area of the court from which the shot is played.

Shot Striking Attitudes

Adopting the correct shot striking attitude for the next shot to be played immediately this is known greatly reduces the amount of time required to hit the shuttle – you arrive in the 'hitting area' prepared! It also ensures the body is carried 'on balance', thus assisting court movement. Essentially you should strike an attitude which incorporates preparatory upper body movement and arm throwing requirements prior to moving towards the shuttle. There are six basic striking attitudes to be practised.

OVERHEAD FOREHAND
(Fig 8)
Right foot towards rear of court and close to the left foot. Right shoulder back with left shoulder towards net – chest parallel with right-hand court side-lines. Racket arm bent with elbow at shoulder level. Racket hand close to head and racket held with loose forehand grip allowing the racket head to fall below shoulder level behind the back. Note the balancing effect of the left hand.

OVERHAND BACKHAND
(Fig 9)
Right foot pointing towards rear of court. Most of back turned to net with left shoulder towards rear of court. Racket arm bent with elbow above shoulder level. Racket hand in front of face, racket held with loose backhand grip allowing racket head to fall to

approximately stomach level. Again note the balancing position of the left hand.

SHOULDER HEIGHT FOREHAND
(Fig 10)
Feet wide apart, in the manner of a fencer's lunge, the right foot forward and pointing at intended point of impact. The racket is held with a loose forehand grip, the arm bent with elbow at shoulder level, racket hand close to right ear to bring racket behind head, the right shoulder pulled back as far as possible. Left hand balances the right.

SHOULDER HEIGHT BACKHAND
(Fig 11)
Feet wide apart, in the manner of a fencer's lunge, the right foot forward and pointing towards intended point of impact. Racket held with a loose backhand grip, racket arm bent with elbow at shoulder level. The racket hand close to the left ear to bring the racket behind head. Right shoulder as far back as possible with most of the back turned to net. Once again the left hand balances the right.

UNDERARM FOREHAND
(Fig 12)
Feet in the extended lunge position, right foot under the right hand. Racket arm bent with elbow down and palm of hand uppermost. Racket held with loose forehand grip allowing cocked hand to bring racket head below level of the hand. Left hand balances out the right.

UNDERARM BACKHAND
(Fig 13)
Feet in extended lunge with right foot across the front of the body. Racket arm bent, the elbow level with but to the right of the hand. Racket held with loose backhand

13

Fig 8   Overhead forehand striking attitude.

Fig 9   Overhead backhand striking attitude.

Fig 10   Shoulder high forehand striking attitude.

Fig 11   Shoulder high backhand striking attitude.

grip, palm downwards with racket head slightly below cocked hand. Again note that the left hand balances out the right.

Movement About Court – Racket Foot Striking
(Fig 14)

The racket foot is, simply, that beneath the racket hand, that is, right for the right-handed player left foot for the left-handed player. Racket foot striking principles of movement are employed by the very skilled players as the most effective and efficient manner of moving rapidly about the court. (The illustrations for bent arm striking also show the racket foot striking principles.) These principles, coupled with shot striking attitudes, ensure that at any point along the path of

travel to the shuttle a 'hitting base' can be made, above or in front of which a shot can be played.

Imagine that from the centre of the court you have to move quickly to cover any of the six areas of the court depicted in Fig 14 to hit a shuttle in front of the body (underarm in the forecourt), to right or left of the body (shoulder level in the mid court), or to hit it from high above the body (overheads in the back court).

Ideally all of the shots would be taken at full 'stretch', at the end of arm throwing and/or arm stretching movements, and on balance both to hit the shuttle and to ensure balanced and rapid recovery thereafter.

Consider the following descriptions in conjunction with Fig 14 bearing in mind that not every conceivable angle of approach

Fig 12   Underarm forehand striking attitude.

Fig 13   Underarm backhand striking attitude.

Fig 14   Movement about court.

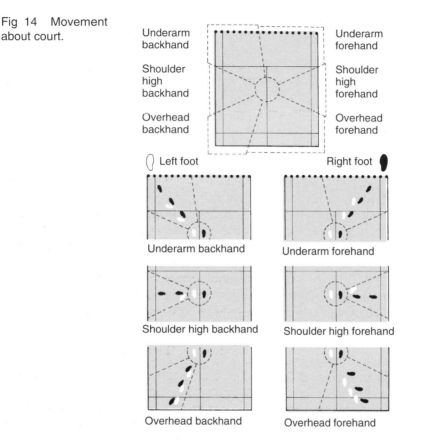

can be sensibly shown. A singles game situation is illustrated but the basic principles of movement about the court are common to all forms of game play. The central circular area is the 'base', a position of readiness applicable, in this instance, to singles play; 'basing' areas for other forms of games play will be considered later. Eventually all of your movements should become smooth, flowing, dynamically balletic – balanced at all times. Initially, however, they should be practised in stages linking one to another until they become a series of 'grooved' instinctive reactions.

There are more 'footprints' than most people will ultimately, perhaps even initially, require. Longer-limbed players will probably need only steps 1, 2 and 5 to cover underarm and shoulder high shots, and possibly only steps 1, 4 and 5 for overhead forehands. The following descriptions allow for the smallest possible number of steps.

To Underarm and Shoulder High Shots

The shuttle will be close to the net or sidelines requiring a long reach. From position of readiness adopt the appropriate shot striking attitude. Prepare to move with a bounce! Up on the toes, bend knees and leap lightly into the air. Land, then take the first short step with the right foot. Bring the other foot up to, but not beyond, this. Now take a long lunge with the racket foot. If the actions were sufficiently dynamic you should have reached a point from which you can hit the shuttle at full arm's stretch and on an extended lunge. After hitting, recover to your original position moving the feet in reverse order. That is, take the racket foot back to the non-racket foot, then step back with the non-racket foot bringing the racket foot back alongside into position of readiness. Or, when strength of legs allows, from the extended lunge hitting position, with one leap pick up both feet and launch backwards (or sideways) into base!

To Above the Head Forehand Shots Towards the Back of the Court

Remember the intention is to hit the shuttle at full arm's upwards reach. To achieve this the feet will need to be close together at point of impact to enable you to hit the shuttle as high as possible above the head. From position of readiness adopt overhead forehand striking attitude. Again with a preparatory bounce, take a short step with the racket foot in line with the intended point of impact. Bring the non-racket foot up to, possibly slightly beyond, the racket foot. Take a longer step back with the racket foot to bring you into the hitting area. Finally bring the non-racket foot alongside the racket foot and hit the shuttle.

Recover by using the follow-after action after hitting to swing the racket foot forward (the stronger the shot the longer the step), step onto the non-racket foot then place both feet quickly into the base area.

To Above the Head Backhand Shots Towards the Back of the Court

Remember the intention is to hit the shuttle at full upward arm's stretch. To achieve this the feet will need to be close together at point of impact to enable you to hit the shuttle as high as possible above the head. From position of readiness adopt overhead backhand striking attitude. Again with the preparatory bounce, swivel the body to face towards the back of the court and take a short step, in line with the intended point of impact, with the racket foot. Step beyond this with the non-racket foot. Take a longer step with the racket foot to bring you into the hitting area. Finally bring the non-racket foot almost alongside the racket foot and hit the shuttle. Recover by taking weight back onto the non-racket foot. Swivel on this foot turning the front of the body back to face the net. No more than two steps should take you back into the base area.

Position of Readiness

This is precisely what the title suggests; a position on the court which allows you to respond quickly and then move to hit the shuttle. Not only is it a physical attitude but, also, an attitude of mind. One has to be ready both mentally and physically, because that is the order of the reaction process, to move rapidly to reach and hit the shuttle. Your weight will be carried easily on the balls of the feet which are placed side by side and about shoulder width apart. The racket head should be carried at about chest level and held loosely. The Movement About Court instructions require you to start with a bounce!

There will be much more on this subject when we consider basing and responding to certain predictable elements of your opponent's abilities.

SUMMARY

Firstly a reminder – in all of the descriptions we have assumed the player to be right-handed. If you are left-handed remember that throughout the narrative you should have substituted left for right and vice versa.

All these elements can, and initially should be, practised separately. They can be practiced without hitting a shuttle to allow you to gain a 'feel' of what is required. Consider all of the elements and your interpretation of these against the illustrations provided. If you do not have a coach to advise and assist you then practise in front of a full-length mirror, with or without racket depending on the amount of room available, to give you a better 'picture' of your interpretation. As with other sports, badminton consists of a large number of small movements which must be blended into a cohesive and graceful whole. Consciously practise each small element, progressively adding one to another, until they become one complete reflex action. You will recall that the elements were, for the best part, presented in reverse order. The correct order for the complete shot making process is as follows. From position of readiness determine the shot to be played and adopt the appropriate stroke striking attitude remembering to take the correct grip. Then travel towards the intended point of impact racket foot striking; hit the shuttle with upper body movement followed by arm throwing followed by hand uncocking followed by follow-after followed by recovery to position of readiness.

With practice you will find that you can reduce these elements to four simpler commands and responses of *prepare – travel – hit – recover.*

2
Serving

Trajectory profiles of the various types of serve are shown in fig 15. They should be considered when each type of serve is discussed.

The serving actions are the only strokes within the game that are controlled by the Laws of Badminton. These are framed in such a manner that they restrict the way in which one serves thereby effectively dictating the serving actions. At time of writing these Laws, stated simply, require that:

1. The shuttle must be served diagonally, i.e. across the centre line of the court, and fall within, or onto, the boundary lines of the receiver's service area.
2. Initial point of contact with the shuttle must be on the base of the shuttle. You may not hit the feathers first or feathers and base together.
3. At the instant of hitting the shuttle no part of the shuttle may be above the server's waist and the head of the racket must be seen to be below the whole of the server's hand holding the racket. You may not hit the shuttle overhand or above the waist but in such a manner that the shuttle's travel is first upwards to pass over the net.
4. The first forward movement of the server's racket constitutes the start of the service, thereafter the serving action must be continuous. You may not make preliminary feints, or once started, stop then restart the service again.
5. It is a fault if the server deliberately delays serving the shuttle in order to obtain

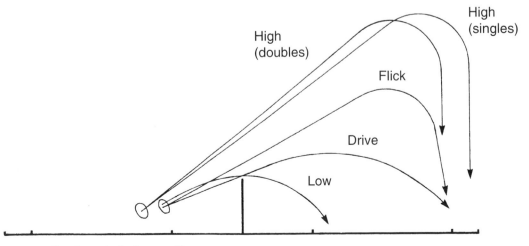

Fig 15   Serving – trajectory profiles.

an unfair advantage. Nor may you serve before the receiver is ready.

6. The server's feet must be within the boundary lines of the service court throughout the serving action. Standing on the service boundary lines is not permitted.

7. Some part of both feet of the server must remain in contact with the surface of the court in a stationary position until the service is delivered. You may not 'walk' into and/or through the serving action. You may however, introduce some degree of weight transfer into your serving action by lifting or lowering some part of each foot to the service action. You may not drag a foot.

8. With the backhand serve there are particular rules regarding 'presentation' which will be addressed when discussing this serve.

As the Laws of Badminton are revised from time to time it is essential that the reader ensures that he is fully aware of the latest interpretation of these.

Serving is the means of starting a rally within the game situation. The Laws allow us to score points only when we are serving. It is imperative, therefore, that the server starts the rally in a manner that enables him (and his partner in the doubles game) to draw from the receiver a response that is more to the server's advantage than the reverse. The Laws of Badminton oblige you to serve in an upwards direction to clear the net, placing you at a disadvantage unless you serve with great accuracy and consistency and variety. Also you must serve with due regard to the receiver's known limitations as defined by the Laws and, eventually, acquired knowledge of a particular receiver's limitations. Bear in mind that the receiver is not permitted to move and must stay within the receiving boundary lines until such time

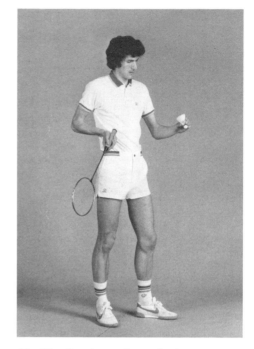

Fig 16 Serving – stance for low forehand action. Note arm bent to bring racket face as high as possible, and hand cocked back.

as the service is delivered (hit). He will wish to avoid lifting the shuttle thus presenting you with the first opportunity to hit down. Not only should he have to cover the probability of you serving low in front of him but also the possibility that you can disguise your intentions and also place the shuttle beyond his immediate reach with variations to your usual serve.

LOW SERVICE

The low service can be played with either a forehand or backhand action. In both cases many of the considerations are the same. Ideally the service should be played in such a manner that the shuttle virtually brushes

Fig 17   Serving – stance for low backhand action. Note elbow up to keep racket head as high as permissible, and hand cocked back.

the net as it passes over to hit the receiver's front service line should it be allowed to fall to the floor. The serving action should be such that, without any change being discernible to the receiver, you can introduce changes of direction, pace, and trajectory.

Reminder – all the following instructions are for right-handed players. If you are left-handed the instructions are the same but 'reverse handed', i.e. for right read left and vice versa.

Forehand Low Service
(Fig 16)

Stand comfortably, feet approximately shoulder width apart, close to the centre line and behind, but close to, the front ser-

vice line. The left foot points in the general direction of the intended flight of the serve with the right foot at approximately right angles to it. The body is erect with the left shoulder just nearer to the net. The shuttle held in the left hand in a manner that allows it, when released, to fall just to the right-hand side of the left foot. The racket is held in a loose forehand grip, arm bent with the elbow tucked close into the waist. The hand is cocked back and downwards to ensure that the racket head is below both hand and waist.

As the shuttle only has to travel a short distance you will not need to 'hit' it. Rather the action will be a gentle 'stroking' of the shuttle – the minimum effort required to propel it across the net to fall just within the receiver's service court area. Without moving the racket arm or 'uncocking' the hand, slowly swivel the upper body by pushing the right hip forward. Do not let the right foot lift or drag along the floor. Release the shuttle by opening the fingers of the left hand just prior to the arrival of the racket, thus gently 'stroking' the shuttle up and over the net to fall into the receiver's service court area.

Backhand Low Service
(Fig 17)

Once again stand comfortably with feet approximately shoulder width apart, close to the centre line and just behind the front service line. This time stand with the right foot forward pointing in the general direction of the service. The left foot is at approximately right angles to the other. The body is erect with the right shoulder very slightly nearer to the net. The shuttle is held with the left hand in a manner that presents the base to the racket face. Hold the racket in a loose backhand grip, arm bent with upper arm almost

21

level with shoulder, hand and racket pointing down; place it against the left hand *not* the shuttle base. You must ensure that the shuttle does not touch the racket as this is a fault. (Check that all of the racket stays below the waist at the intended point of impact.) Without allowing the shuttle to move take the racket back by cocking the hand then, without pausing, uncock the hand, release the shuttle and gently 'stroke' it over the net.

Notes On Low Service

Do not be deterred if you fail to strike the shuttle initially as timing the release of the shuttle to coincide with the racket swing requires some practice. When you have co-ordinated shuttle release with racket swing and succeeded in putting racket to shuttle with some consistency you will discover that the shuttle has done one of a number of things. It may have passed over the net, the skirt of the shuttle gently brushing the tape as it does so, and fallen onto the line of, or just within, the receiver's service court area. If so change nothing about your serving action but repeat it until the movement becomes 'grooved' to the point that you can do it, quite literally, with your eyes closed.

More likely you will not have achieved this initial success but find that the shuttle will have done one of the following:

1. Failed to clear the net.
2. Travelled over the net but was too high and fell short of the receiver's line.
3. Was too high and travelled too far into the receiver's area.
4. Passed over the net and was of a good length but fell into the other court area.

ADJUSTMENTS

Shuttle constantly hits the net *(Figs 18 & 19)* Try standing nearer to the net without altering any part of your serving action. Or alter the angle of the cocked hand – from broken to solid line as in the illustrations. Or try a combination of both.

Shuttle travels too high and falls short of the line *(Figs 18 & 19)* Try standing further away from the net without altering any other part of your action. Or alter the angle of the cocked hand – from solid to broken line as in the illustrations. Or try a combination of both. Are you hitting rather than stroking the shuttle? Are you 'uncocking' the hand too much? Have you straightened the racket arm so that the racket is too low at point of impact thus sending the shuttle higher?

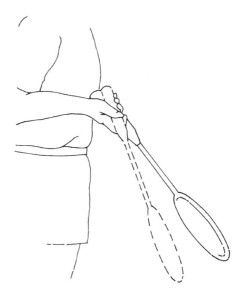

Fig 18 Forehand low serve cocked hand attitudes.

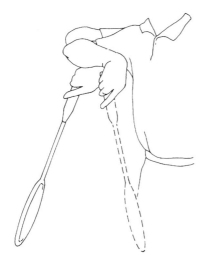

Fig 19   Backhand low serve cocked hand attitudes.

Shuttle travels too high and too far
Consider the first, third and fourth suggestions under 'Shuttle too high and falls short'.

Shuttle falls into wrong court Assuming that the serve was otherwise acceptable, without changing any other element of the action experiment with changing the direction of your stance.

Low Service Variations

Practise the low service from and to both of the service court areas as there are small differences to be perfected. It is recommended that, ultimately, you should perfect both the forehand and backhand methods of serving. Mention was made earlier of the need to 'groove' the action to the point that you can low serve, quite literally, with your eyes closed. This was no exaggeration as the ability to serve with great accuracy and consistency must become one of the strongest elements of your game.

Obviously one cannot always use the basic (straight towards centre line) low serve without it becoming predictable and therefore exploitable by the receiver. So that the receiver should not constantly anticipate your basic low service, moving quickly to take this near the top of its flight, you will need to add variety to create a repertoire of low serves. This takes a number of forms. In all cases the variation must be *added* to your basic low serving action. If you are to catch the receiver unawares you must give him no early warning of your intentions. These additions will be achieved by 'playing' slightly different 'tunes' with the fingers on a loosely held racket.

Let us assume that, as a result of diligent practice, you have achieved near perfection with a grooved basic low serve. The shuttle leaves the racket on a low trajectory and skims the net to fall just within the receiving court close to the centre line. If you use this serve most of the time you must employ the occasional variation, both to overcome the predictability of your basic serve and/or to catch the receiver unawares.

Angled Serves
(Figs 20 & 21)

OBJECTIVE
To convince the receiver that your low serve will be straight to its usual place then to serve wide of his racket, thus making him miss the shuttle or take it later than he would wish.

METHOD
Without any change to your basic grooved action, add a slightly angled racket face by 'rolling' the racket softly with the fingers to direct the shuttle to the left or right of its usual flight path. Looking down on your

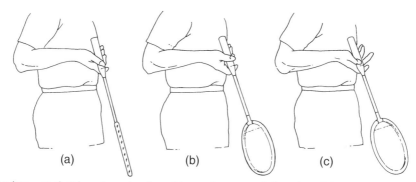

Fig 20   Serving – racket head angles to achieve changes of direction; (a) straight serve; (b) angled low serve (from right to left); (c) angled low serve (from left to right).

racket: holding the inside edge forward will angle the shuttle to your right (Fig 20c); holding the inside edge back will angle the shuttle to your right (Fig 20b); either way, the shuttles are sent towards the outside boundary lines of the receiver's front line. Use 20c when serving from the left court and 20b from the right court. Be mindful that the 'stroking' actions need to be slightly stronger as the shuttles have further to travel.

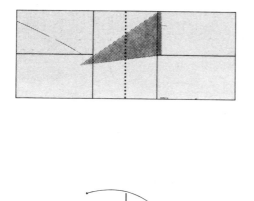

Fig 21   Target area for angled low serves.

Flick Serves
(Figs 22 & 23)

OBJECTIVE
To convince the receiver that he will have to receive your basic low serve only to have the shuttle 'flicked' over his head and beyond his immediate reach to achieve either an outright winner or dramatically reduce his response time so he produces only a poor return. In any event you should oblige him to play from further back in court than he might wish.

METHOD
Flicks must be just higher than the immediate upwards reach of the receiver's stretched arm and racket. They may be played to the right or the left of, as well as immediately over the head of, the receiver to fall just within the back area of his receiving area (*see* Fig 15), calling for a quite strong action.
  For the forehand, without changing your basic low serve add the flick action by quickly tightening your grip on a loosely held racket – snap the racket back into the palm with the last three fingers. Ensure that the racket head is still below the hand and

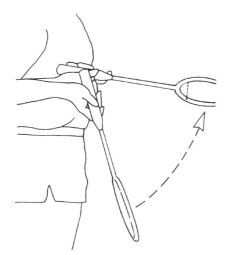

Fig 22   Forehand flick service action.

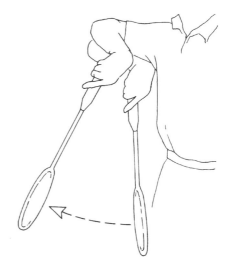

Fig 23   Backhand flick service action.

not above the waist at impact point.

For the backhand, without changing the basic low serve add the flick action by quickly changing from a soft 'stroking' to a sharp 'tapping' action – think about hitting with the finger nails! Be very careful not to hit with the racket above hand and/or waist. Trajectories will be much flatter than are possible with the forehand.

Drive Serves
(Fig 24)

OBJECTIVE
To convince the receiver that he is about to receive your basic low serve and then 'driving' the shuttle past him. Aim to either beat him completely or reduce his response time so that he plays only a poor return.

METHOD
Drives should not be higher than the receiver's immediate upwards stretch. Rather the trajectory should be such that the shuttle travels beneath the receiver's racket and

just above his shoulder. They can be played to the right or left of the receiver to fall anywhere within his service court area. (It is extremely difficult, if not impossible, for this form of service to be played off the backhand serving action without striking the shuttle above the waist – a service fault – so we are considering only the forehand version.) Without change to the basic low serve action, push the heel of the racket hand rapidly forward immediately prior to hitting, uncocking the hand slightly when doing so. This action is added to the basic serving action.

Word of Warning

There is a danger that you may 'declare your intentions' to the receiver by slightly altering the preparations for the service variations or swinging/pushing too quickly too soon. Remember that the actions should be added to your basic service action. More importantly, you run the risk of introducing faults into your service action by

25

employing preliminary feints, striking the shuttle above your waist and/or your hand (particularly with the backhand serve) and stopping and then restarting the serving action.

Sliced Serves
(Fig 25)

Stated simply, slicing actions spin the shuttle during some part of its flight and can influence its pace, direction and trajectory. Slice can be introduced into most forms of low serving. It can also be used, as an alternative to those already stated, to lower the trajectory of the basic low serve. Applied correctly it will induce curved flights to the shuttle trajectory. Generally slices tend to slow the pace of the shuttle, therefore the serving action speed should be increased. Slices are obtained by a slight pushing forward action of the racket while at the same time 'drawing' the strings across the base of the shuttle away from the intended flight path. To direct the shuttle to the left the slic-

ing action is from left to right. Right to left action sends the shuttle to the right. The slicing principle can be applied to virtually all of the low serve variations.

Generally low serve variations are used less often than basic low serves. This does not mean that they need less practice. Such are the advantages to be gained from these when played that they must be perfect. Perfection is gained only as a result of constant, high-quality practice.

HIGH SERVICE

Very seldom are high serves used in doubles games. This is not to suggest that they may or should not be used for they are useful against the comparative beginner. However, they feature little at advanced levels of doubles play and we will consider them only for singles play when the high service is used a great deal, very often to the total exclusion of the low serve and its variations.

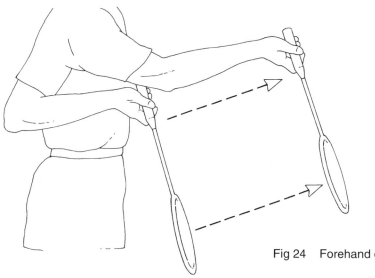

Fig 24   Forehand drive service action.

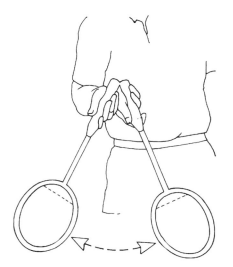

Fig 25   Low service slicing action.

when allowed to drop it falls to the right and just in front of the left foot. The racket is held in a loose forehand grip, racket head up and behind racket foot.

The shuttle has to travel a great distance, first up into the air then to fall onto or very near the back service line. It will require a powerful hitting action to achieve this result. Swing the racket down and forward, release the shuttle and hit it up and forward uncocking the hand as you do so. Follow after along the intended flight of the shuttle with the racket and by thrusting the right hip powerfully forward. Do not let your foot come off, or drag along, the floor!

As with the low serve do not be deterred if you miss the shuttle initially. Practise

The objective is to place the shuttle into the back of the receiver's service court area after it has reached sufficient height (which may be limited on occasions by low ceilings) to fall vertically straight down. This has the twofold effect of making the opponent play shots from the greatest distances away from your fore, mid and back court areas, and making him deal with a vertically falling shuttle. The trajectories are indicated in Fig 15. Only the forehand serving action is considered as backhands cannot sensibly be played.

METHOD
(Figs 26–8)
Stand comfortably, feet slightly more than shoulder width apart, close to the centre line, and nearer to the front service line than the back. The left foot points in the general direction of the intended flight of the service, the right foot is at approximately right angles to this. Body erect, left shoulder towards net, shuttle held so that

Fig 26   High service preparation.
Comfortable stance, arm back and hand cocked.

27

Fig 27　High service swing. Shuttle just about to be struck and hand about to be uncocked.

Fig 28　High service follow-after. Powerful follow-after with arm projected in direction of shuttle.

shuttle release and arm swing until you have co-ordinated these. Once you have co-ordinated all of the actions (it may take longer than the low serve action) you will see that your serve has done one of a number of things.

It may have travelled as high as the roof level allows and fallen onto, or very close to, the back service line. If so, change nothing but practise constantly until the action is totally 'grooved'.

More likely, you will not have had this initial success but find that the shuttle has done one of the following:

1. Travelled high but fell short of the back receiving line.
2. Had a flat trajectory and fell outside the back receiving line.
3. Was high and of good length but fell into the wrong service court area or outside the side-line of the receiving court area.

ADJUSTMENTS
Shuttle falls short Try serving from nearer to the net. Did you uncock the hand too strongly? Did you remember to keep the momentum going by following the direction of your service with the racket hand?

Trajectory flat and too long Try standing further back and put more emphasis into hitting the shuttle upwards. Was the hand uncocked sufficiently?

Shuttle out of the side of the court or into the wrong court area Change nothing but the position of your feet to alter the direction of your serving stance.

High Service Variations

Practise the high service from and to both receiving court areas as there are small differences in attitude to be perfected. You are reminded, once again, that unless you can serve well you will be unable to score points, therefore grooving your service action to achieve great accuracy and consistency is essential.

There are a limited number of variations that can be played off the high serve action. You should explore your opponent's reactions to serves directed to various points along the back receiving line from just inside (or on) the centre line to just inside (or on) the outside boundary line. From time to time a faster serve with a flatter trajectory, still aimed at the back line, could be introduced to unsettle the receiver's responses. You can try a low serve played off the high serve action. Be careful that you do not contravene the Laws regarding preliminary feints and/or stopping and restarting the service action. All of the possible variations should be practised as much as the basic action. You may only use them occasionally but when you do they must be effective.

SUMMARY

All service actions are subject to the Laws of Badminton. You must be aware of these and ensure that all of your serves stay well within the restrictions imposed.

Serves are one of the ways, if not the most important, of promoting a rally which will end in your favour. Only if you can win rallies while you are serving can you score points. If you cannot serve well, you stand very little chance of winning. It is essential that you perfect all of your serving actions, basic and variations, to achieve this end.

Only good practice makes perfect. Serving requires feeling and an unhurried approach. Twelve unhurried good practice serves are of more value than twice that number of rushed, inaccurate attempts.

3

Shot Making

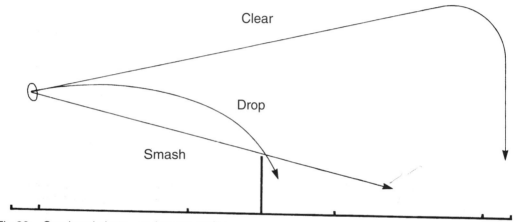

Fig 29 Overhead shots – trajectory profiles.

Trajectory profiles of the various shots to be described under each stroke group heading are shown in diagrammatic form at the beginning of each section. Only one profile for each shot in the group is shown, as to present a comprehensive range of all the possibilities would lead to confusion. Profiles shown can also be considered as 'angled' shots, i.e., they can be played cross-court as well as straight.

The elements of basic stroke making have already been dealt with in some detail. They are repeated by providing a detailed stroke cycle at the beginning of descriptions for each group of shots. Thereafter these same basics are employed for each of the shots in the group. It is essential that all

your movements right up to the moment of hitting the shuttle are produced in an identical manner thus introducing disguise and deception from the outset. Only as you actually hit the shuttle should your opponent be able to determine which shot out of the strokes group you have selected. Each specific shot then has a description and illustrations of the actual hitting of the shuttle and follow-after, an example of one simple practice and then additional comment regarding any corrections required, variations, and so on.

Reminder – all shot descriptions are for right-handed players. If you are left-handed then read left for right and vice versa.

Fig 30 Overhead forehand clear – preparation. Position of readiness prior to moving to take the shuttle.

Fig 31 Movement to striking position. Moving back 'racket foot striking'.

Fig 32 Striking attitude. Body underneath and just behind the intended point of impact.

Fig 33 Hand cocking action. Upper arm being thrown and hand starting to uncock.

Fig 34   Hitting. Point of impact just in front of head, taken at full stretch and hand uncocked fully.

Fig 35   Racket follow-after. Follow after in upwards and forwards direction.

Fig 36   Body follow-after. Right shoulder being carried forward pulling right foot up and forward.

Fig 37   Recovery. Recovery back to base being completed by moving forward naturally.

FOREHAND SHOTS ABOVE THE HEAD
(Fig 29)

The **stroke cycle** for all of these shots is as follows.

1. **Prepare**, with a small bounce on the balls of the toes, and adopt the appropriate
2. **Stroke striking atttitude**, upper body rotated so that right shoulder is back, racket arm bent with elbow at about shoulder level, racket hand close to head holding racket in loose forehand grip allowing racket head to fall below shoulder level, left hand in counter-balance, then ...
3. **Travel**, racket foot 'striking', i.e., right foot always in advance of the left, using the short left–long right step principle of moving, into the ...
4. **Hitting area** directly behind the shuttle in a position in which, if you chose, you could catch the shuttle in your still raised left hand then ...
5. **Hit** the shuttle by driving the right shoulder up and forwards followed by vigorous arm throwing. As the arm straightens, enabling the shuttle to be struck at full arm's stretch, uncock the hand and tighten grip simultaneously, allowing hand, upper body and right foot to ...
6. **Follow after** the shuttle along the trajectory of, and at the pace of, the particular shot selected to finally ...
7. **Recover** to position of readiness thus completing the stroke cycle.

Overhead Forehand – Clear
(Figs 30 –37)

OBJECTIVE
To hit the shuttle high to the rear area of the opposite court ideally to fall straight down vertically on, or close to, the very back line, obliging the opponent to play from the very back of his rear court. The shot is used constantly in the singles game, less frequently in doubles play.

METHOD
The hitting point will be above and just in front of the head. Use a powerful punching action to hit very strongly up and forward. Follow-after is such that it has the effect of lifting the right foot up and forward to become the first recovery step to the position of readiness for the opponent's response.

SIMPLE PRACTICE
First 'shadow' the total sequence of movements to become familiar with all of these – use this as a short warm-up. Then stand in the hitting position while another player hits a shuttle high into your rear court by practising his high serve. Do not hit the shuttle initially but catch it in your left hand to check that you are in the correct hitting position. Now start practising just the hitting, follow-after and first recovery step forward elements. Do not be deterred by any initial failures to make contact. This is a co-ordination problem and needs practice. After a while you will have co-ordinated your movements (do not compromise the movement sequence) to coincide with the arrival of the shuttle. At this stage you can start making judgments regarding overall results and effect any necessary corrections as follows.

ADJUSTMENTS
Shuttle leaves the racket with a sharp impact sound, travels high into the air and falls vertically on, or close within, the very back boundary line. Change nothing and continue practising until the action becomes totally 'grooved'.

Shuttle travels too high and falls short
A possible subsidiary effect may be that the right foot is not lifted by the hitting action. Check impact point – is this just in front of the body? Is follow-after aimed up and *at* a point directly above the opponent's back line?

Shuttle has a flat trajectory and falls short You may have to consider the reverse of the above corrections. Is the impact point too far in front of the body, with the result that your follow-after is forward rather than up? Have you under-hit? The hitting action must be fast, strong, up and forward – a powerful punch; draw shoulder back before throwing the arm.

Shuttle travels in the wrong direction
Assuming that all of the other elements are basically correct, check that the correct (forehand) grip is maintained at the actual moment of hitting? Are both hand and racket head being thrown along the intended trajectory of the shuttle?

NOTE
When attempting to make one correction very often another element breaks down. Do not be too dismayed by this but methodically practise until the results are as near as possible to perfection. Above all ensure that the results are effective – you obtain the result for which you have aimed; and efficient – you feel comfortable and are not compromising the next elements of full recovery to your base.

COMPLETING THE STROKE CYCLE
Now start practising movements to and from the hitting position – the travel and recovery elements. Progress in stages. From a position one long step away from the hitting position, adopt the striking attitude, take a step back into the hitting area, hit and recover one step forward. Practise this a number of times: step back – hit the shuttle – step forward. When comfortable with the situation progressively increase the number of travel and recovery steps until the stroke cycle is complete. You start from and finish in a position of readiness!

Following this, practise the entire stroke cycle but now hitting cross-court clears. Hit the shuttle diagonally from one corner to the other. For both right to left and vice versa the main requirement is the same. Ensure you have adopted the striking attitude, with the right shoulder back prepared to hit before travelling back otherwise you may have trouble both with travelling and hitting. Follow-after is even more strongly in the direction of the position from which you wish to make your opponent play as the shuttle has to travel slightly further.

It is essential to perfect the basic overhead forehand clear action. In perfecting this by using the correct and complete stroke cycle you later employ this action to 'add' other different hits and follow-after actions to produce smashes and drops. All these overhead forehand shots will become the mainstay of your game.

Overhead Forehand – Smash
(Figs 38 & 39)

OBJECTIVE
To hit shuttles extremely quickly and steeply down into the opponent's midcourt area, either at, in front of, or to left or right of him in order to score an outright winner or draw a poor upwards-directed response. It is used extensively in all forms of games play.

Fig 38   Overhead smash – hitting. Note point of impact positively in front of the body – compare this with Fig 34.

Fig 39   Overhead forehand smash – racket follow-after. Compare this with Fig 35 and note the emphasis on downwards follow-after.

METHOD

All preparatory elements up to the moment of hitting are exactly as for the overhead forehand clear. The point of impact is immediately above, as for clears. But now, because the intended trajectory is as steeply down as possible but still has to clear the net, the point of impact is more in front of the head than for the clear. The hitting action is very powerfully down and at the intended area of the opponent's court. The operative word is 'throw'! Throw shoulder and heel of hand at the impact point, uncock the hand fiercely, tighten the grip sharply to increase the racket head speed greatly. Throw the racket head, metaphorically not literally, along the intended trajec-

tory, which is out in front of you and over the net. These powerful first upward (to give maximum height extension therefore angled downward trajectory) and then forward movements should lift the foot off the floor to become the first step of recovery to base and position of readiness.

Without hitting the shuttle 'warm up' by shadowing the entire stroke cycle a number of times. Exaggerate the throwing of arm, hand, racket and follow-after to produce a dramatic forwards-projected 'swish' from the racket. This action should be so fast forward that you are obliged to put the right foot out in front to maintain balance.

35

SIMPLE PRACTICE

Stand in a position near the back of the court. Another player practises either his doubles high or flick serve to feed the shuttle to you. Do not hit the shuttle initially but let it fall to the floor. It should fall in front of your left (forward) foot. Start by practising the forward swing, hitting, follow-after and first recovery step elements of the stroke cycle. As point of impact, racket head speed and follow-after differ from those for the clear timing may suffer, leading to an initial failure to connect. Once these different elements are timed to coincide with arrival of the shuttle, practise a number of smashes. Take great care to direct the shuttle away from the feed so as not to cause injury to him from a heavily struck shuttle. He should serve diagonally thus allowing you to hit straight smashes. Use these early attempts to make judgments regarding the results and effect any necessary corrections as follows.

ADJUSTMENTS

The shuttle leaves the racket with a very sharp impact sound, travels extremely quickly over the net with a steep trajectory, to land in the opponent's mid-court and hit the floor hard. Change nothing but continue practicing until the action is grooved.

Shuttle has a flat trajectory The shuttle leaves the racket with a very sharp impact sound but travels flat to land in the back court. Is your point of impact slightly too far back? Have you followed down rather than after the shuttle? Have you stretched to maximum upwards reach before hitting forward?

Shot is fast but into the net Is the point of impact too far in front of the body? Have you followed down rather than after the shuttle? Have you stretched up to maximum upwards reach before hitting forward?

Shuttle travels in the wrong direction Assuming that all other elements are basically correct, have you checked to ensure the correct forehand grip is maintained at the moment of hitting? Did the racket hand, therefore the racket head, follow after the intended direction of the shot?

Once you are consistently achieving an acceptable result move on to practise the entire stroke cycle – prepare – travel – hit – recover, as described for the clear. Then go on to practise cross-court forehand smashes from both right and left back corners of the court.

Overhead Forehand – Drop

OBJECTIVE

To hit the shuttle in an apparently powerful manner, only for it to fall gently over and steeply down the net into the opponent's fore court. If played correctly, that is, deceptively (with apparent force but gentle flight) to catch the opponent unawares thus either beating him completely or forcing a late hit response. Used extensively in all forms of games play.

METHOD

The shot can be played off either the clear or smash actions. The slow drop is played off the clear action when the shuttle trajectory will tend to be initially upwards, then down to fall steeply down and close to the net. For fast drops the smash action is used. The trajectory is then flatter and the shuttle falls further into the opponent's court. All preparatory elements up to moment of hitting and points of impact are exactly as for the appropriate overhead forehand shot. For the slow drop the observing opponent will see a hitting action which is very powerfully upwards. If the fast drop is played the opponent will see a hitting action which is powerfully forwards. The operative word is deception! The opponent is deceived into believing that either your clear or smash action is being played only to be caught out by a slow or fast drop. The results are produced by very late conversion of 'tight fist' into 'open fingers' shots – they are light touch shots!

SIMPLE PRACTICE

The following instruction relates to drops played off either the clear or smash action. Both should be practised straight and cross-court. Have another player feed shuttles in the ways described earlier. The prepare – travel – hit – recover cycle of events must be identical to whichever shot is practised, clear for slow drops or smash for fast drops. The only changes will be to point of impact, racket head speed and follow-after.

FOR FAST DROP OFF THE SMASH ACTION

The point of impact wiill be above and positively in front of the body, as for the smash. The initial hitting action, very apparent to the opponent, is fast until *immediately* prior to hitting the shuttle, when it is slowed dramatically. The shuttle leaves the racket in a flat, slower than smash, trajectory (follow-after continues strongly forward to maintain the illusion) to land between the back of forecourt/front of mid-court areas of the opponent's court.

FOR SLOW DROP OFF THE CLEAR ACTION

The point of impact will be above and in front of the body, as for the clear. The initial hitting action, very apparent to the opponent, is fast upwards until *immediately* prior to hitting, when it is slowed dramatically. The shuttle leaves the racket in a gentle upwards trajectory (follow-after continues upwards and forward to maintain the illusion) to fall steeply down close to the net into the opponent's forecourt area.

It should be particularly noted that it is essential to develop the technique of 'dramatically slowing' the throwing actions. It is all too easy to play the two different shots by using slower, obviously different, hitting techniques. The objective is to create illusions, the opponent 'seeing' one shot only to receive another.

ADJUSTMENTS

Shuttle leaves the racket in the desired manner and achieves exactly the result described above. Furthermore, when viewing the shots being played, the feed is deceived, by the late changes in the hitting actions, into believing that the other, more powerful shots, had been played. Change nothing and continue practising until both of the actions become grooved.

Shuttle travels too high and/or too far
The speed of the racket head was not slowed sufficiently; the hand has been uncocked too strongly. Do not alter the fast build-ups but, with persistent practice, learn to slow the hand action at precisely the correct time to obtain the results required.

Good results are obtained but at the expense of disguise and deception This is the area where your feed can positively assist you. He is able to advise you that the good results were only obtained because all of the elements were slowed down. He was not deceived, realising from the outset that the drops were about to be played. If so practise again, this time with your normal shot-making actions, accepting that, initially, the drops may be too high or too far into the opponent's court. Practise until your quick actions produce slow results.

The drops fail to reach and/or clear the net Assuming that you employed the fast build-ups have you slowed the hand action too dramatically – have you over-acted? Continue practising once again, referring to the other notes above as results improve.

Initially it is preferable that you over-hit the drops rather than not have them go over the net. Bear in mind that the first essential is to keep the shuttle in play – no points are awarded for 'almost succeeding' in making the shuttle pass over the net! Like serves, drops require 'feeling', a sense of touch which will only be acquired by constant practice.

Once you are consistently achieving acceptable results move on to practise the entire stroke cycle – prepare – travel – hit – recover. Then go on to practise the cross-courts.

BACKHAND SHOTS ABOVE THE HEAD
(Fig 29)

The stroke cycle for all of these shots is as follows.
1. **Prepare**, with a small bounce on the balls of the toes, and adopt the appropriate...
2. **Stroke striking atttitude**, upper body

rotated so that most of the back is exposed to the net, racket arm bent with elbow above shoulder level, racket hand in front of face holding racket in loose backhand grip allowing racket head to fall below shoulder level, left hand in counter-balance, then ...
3. **Travel**, racket foot 'striking', i.e., right foot always in advance of the left, using the short left–long right step principle of moving, into the ...
4. **Hitting area** directly behind the shuttle; it is between you and the net, in a position in which the shuttle would fall down the right-hand side of your back if allowed to drop, then ...
5. **Hit** the shuttle by employing some (the amount is limited) upper body twisting of the shoulders, then with a powerful movement of the right shoulder, upper and forearm muscles (in that order) throw the hand over the elbow to maximum upwards reach uncocking the hand and tightening grip simultaneously, then ...
6. **Follow after** the shuttle. The follow-after is limited since, if executed correctly, both shoulder and elbow will have 'locked' at moment of hitting, but it will be along the intended trajectory of, and at the pace of, the particular shot selected ...
7. **Recover** by stepping back onto the non-racket foot. Swivel on this and swing the other towards the net. Complete the turn by a further small swivel on the racket foot. Move forward naturally to complete the stroke cycle.

Overhead Backhand – Clear
(Figs 40–47)

OBJECTIVE
To hit the shuttle high to the rear area of the opposite court ideally to fall straight down vertically on, or close to, the very back line,

obliging the opponent to play from the very back of his rear court. The shot is used constantly in the singles game; less frequently in doubles play.

METHOD

Point of impact is above and just behind the right shoulder, that is, between the back and the net. The hitting action is powerfully upwards and along the intended trajectory of the shuttle. This powerful upwards movement is such that your weight is lifted onto the tips of the toes. Follow-after is limited to the racket head. Do not attempt to follow after with the hand and/or arm or attempt to make hitting part of the recovery movement. Having played the shot, immediately recover to the position of readiness.

SIMPLE PRACTICE

Rehearse the movements a number of times to warm the body. Stand towards the back of the court, the backhand (left) side, with heels close to the centre line – toes pointing towards the side-lines, right shoulder towards net, so that you see the on–coming shuttle when fed. Have the 'feed' strike a high service directed just inside the side-lines; it will help considerably if he feeds from an angle which allows you to keep the shuttle in sight throughout its flight. Do not hit the shuttle initially but take a step with the right foot into the striking position and let the shuttle fall to the floor. The shuttle should have fallen onto or just behind the right shoulder – between your shoulder and the net. Now practise the shot by stepping and hitting the shuttle. This may require a great deal of practice before you manage to hit particularly as, to produce the best results, you will lose sight of the shuttle momentarily. Under no circumstances be deterred by initial failure to hit the shuttle

very hard. Your first attempts need only produce gentle shots, provided always that the shuttle travels upwards and you employ the correct action. Progressively, as your sense of timing improves, hit the shuttle harder, up and further into the other side of the court. Remember that the emphasis must be on sharply throwing the hand upwards to 'lock' the shoulder and arm joints. By this stage you should be able to make judgments regarding the results being obtained. Any corrections that may be necessary can be made as follows.

ADJUSTMENTS

Shuttle leaves the racket with a sharp impact sound, travels high into the air and falls vertically on, or very near to, the back boundary line. Change nothing and continue practising until the actions become 'grooved'.

Shuttle travels too high and falls short A possible subsidiary effect is that body weight is more towards the rear of the court than the net. Would the shuttle, had you not hit it, have fallen between you and the back lines? Check impact point – you may need to be further back in the court. Did you throw the hand strongly enough? Was the arm fully extended at moment of impact?

The shuttle has a flat trajectory and falls short Check the impact point again – do you need to be nearer to the shuttle as you hit? The hitting action must be fast, strong and upwards. The upper arm must be thrown and the hand uncocked strongly.

Shuttle travels in the wrong direction Have you the correct backhand grip on the racket at actual point of impact? If the shuttle fell out of the court on your side was this

Fig 40   Overhead backhand clear –
preparation. Position of readiness prior to
moving to hit the shuttle.

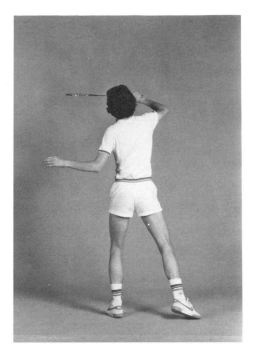

Fig 41   Movement to hitting position.
Moving back 'racket foot striking'.

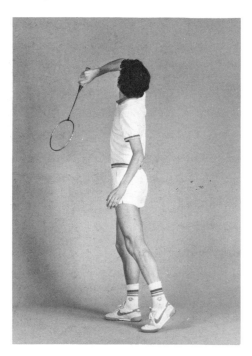

Fig 42   Striking attitude. Body underneath
and just behind (relative to position on
court) intended point of impact.

Fig 43   Hand action. Upper arm being
thrown and hand starting to uncock.

Fig 44 Hitting. Point of impact just behind head, at full stretch with hand fully uncocked.

Fig 45 Racket follow-after. Having hit in a positively upwards direction, follow-after is restricted to uncocking hand only.

Fig 46 Body follow-after. Right shoulder and right foot being turned towards net and base.

Fig 47 Recovery. Recovery back to base being completed by moving forward naurally.

41

because too much of the back had been turned to the net? Conversely, did the shuttle travel across the court because too little of the back was turned?

Having corrected as many faults as possible with minimal foot movement, continue practising but now with movement from and then back to 'base' (position of readiness) in the manner described under overhead forehand. In addition to practising the straight clear you should also try the cross-court clear. There is just the one – from your backhand corner into the opponent's backhand corner. What there is of follow-after must be in the intended direction of the shot. As the shuttle has to travel further the action will be much stronger.

The basic clear action will be the basis for all of the overhead backhand shots. It must be perfected, which will require considerable time – probably far more than for the forehand shots. By perfecting this action you will later be able to employ disguise and deception by 'adding' different follow-afters and impact strengths to produce smashes and drops.

Overhead Backhand – Smash
(Fig 48 & 49)

OBJECTIVE
To strike the shuttle extremely quickly and very steeply down into the opposing mid-court at, in front of or to either side of the opponent, if not to beat him completely then to draw a weak lifted response. Can be used in all forms of games play.

METHOD
Point of impact will be above your right shoulder and positively between back and net. The hitting effort will be down as a result of the hand, and racket, being vigorously uncocked over the top of the wrist. Follow-after, which as a result of the joints 'locking-up' is very limited, must be powerfully and positively down. Whilst the shuttle must be taken at maximum upwards reach – to give the steepest downwards trajectory – you should be very aware of having your weight down on the right foot unlike the clear, which is uplifting.

SIMPLE PRACTICE
Take up the same attitude as for the clear simple practice but much nearer to the net, in the mid-court. The feed must serve loosely, that is, not too high or too far down the court. As always, let the shuttle fall to the floor a number of times to become familar with the impact point. The shuttle should fail to reach the back of your shoulder. Practise only one step and hitting. Point of impact and follow-after emphasis have been changed so there may again be an initial failure to connect. Once the slightly different timing has been co-ordinated practise a number of smashes. Take care to have the shuttle fed diagonally so that the smash, hit straight, is away from the feed. From these early practices make judgments regarding the results and make any necessary corrections as follows.

ADJUSTMENTS
Shuttle leaves the racket with a sharp impact sound, travelling quickly over the net with a steep downwards trajectory, to fall sharply into the opponent's mid-court area. Change nothing and continue practising until the actions become grooved.

Shuttle has a flat trajectory falling close to or passing over the back boundary line. Did you put enough emphasis into strongly forc-

Fig 48   Overhead backhand smash –
striking. Note point of impact positively
behind right shoulder – compare this with
Fig 44.

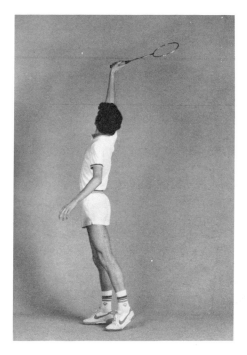

Fig 49   Overhead smash – racket
follow- after. Compare this with Fig 45
and note emphasis on downwards
follow-after.

ing the follow-after action of upper arm, hand and racket down the intended trajectory? Were you too near point of impact? Did you hit from a high enough point – at full arm's stretch?

Shuttle travels into the net Are you too far behind the shuttle? Is the shuttle being taken at full arm upwards stretch or too low?

Shuttle travels in wrong direction Check to ensure that the correct backhand grip is being maintained at actual moment of impact. Have you turned the back too much or too little? Turning too much will send the shuttle out of court on your side. Turning too little is not as serious as the shuttle

should still fall into the opponent's court as an angled smash!

When you have achieved a consistent result, move on to practising the entire sequence of prepare – travel – hit – recover as described earlier. From that point move on to practise deliberately produced cross-court smashes. There is just one – from your backhand side to the opponent's back-hand side.

Overhead Backhand – Drop

OBJECTIVE
To hit the shuttle in an apparently powerful manner, only for it to fall gently over and

steeply down the net into the opponent's forecourt. If played correctly, i.e. deceptively (with apparent force but gentle flight) this will catch the opponent unawares, thus either beating him completely or forcing a late hit response. Used extensively in all forms of game.

METHOD

The shots can be played off either the clear or smash actions. If played off the clear action the flight will be slower, the trajectory initially upwards after leaving the racket, the shuttle falling steeply down and close to the net. When played off the smash action the shuttle will travel faster, the trajectory will be flatter and the shuttle will fall further into the opponent's forecourt. In both cases the opponents should be convinced, by your preliminary build-up, that either the clear or smash is about to be played. You should have disguised your intentions and deceived your opponents!

SIMPLE PRACTICES

Proceed in the manner already described for the forehand overhead drops.

For slow drops off the clear action, the point of impact will be precisely the same as that for the clear action. The hand uncocking action will be faster until *immediately* prior to hitting the shuttle when it will be slowed dramatically. The shuttle will leave the racket in a gentle upwards trajectory to fall steeply down close to the net.

For fast drops off the smash action, the point of impact will be precisely the same as that for the smash action. The hand is uncocked very quickly initially up to *immediately* prior to hitting the shuttle, when it will be slowed dramatically. The shuttle leaves the racket with a flattish trajectory to pass close to the top of the net and fall

close to the back edge of the opponent's forecourt.

As with the forehead overhead drops the operative words are that 'the hand uncocking action will be fast until immediately before striking'. Remember that your objective is to disguise your intentions and deceive the opponent.

ADJUSTMENTS

Shuttles leave the racket in the manners described and achieve exactly the required results. Furthermore, when viewing the shots being played, the feed is deceived by your disguised actions into believing that the other, more powerful, shots had been played. Change nothing and continue practising until both of the actions become grooved.

Shuttle travels too high and/or too far
The speed of the hand action, and therefore racket head was not slowed soon enough. Do not alter the initial fast racket head action but, with persistent practice, learn to slow it at precisely the correct time to obtain the results required.

Good results are obtained but at the expense of disguise and deception This is the area where, once again, your feed can offer positive assistance. Is he able to detect your intention to play the drops because of your very different and slow actions? Should this be the case, then practise again, this time with the faster clear and smash actions slowed dramatically to produce the drops. Continue the practices, referring to the above notes as results improve.

The drops fail to reach and/or clear the net Assuming that you are employing fast

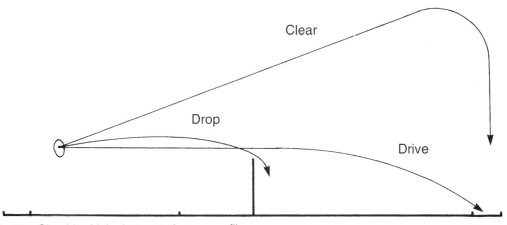

Fig 50   Shoulder high shots – trajectory profiles.

build-ups, have you slowed the hand action too dramatically? Continue practising once again referring to the other notes as results improve.

It is preferable that initially you over-hit the drops to positively clear the net. With continuous practice you then learn to play the shots tighter and tighter to the net. As with the serves and the forehand overhead drops, backhand drops, most particularly, require feeling, and this sense of touch will only be acquired by constant practice.

SHOULDER HIGH SHOTS
(Fig 50)

1. **Prepare**, with a small bounce on the balls of the toes, and adopt the appropriate ...
2. **Stroke striking attitude**, either shoulder high forehand or backhand striking attitude appropriate to the shot to be played.
3. **Travel**, 'racket foot striking', i.e., right foot always in advance of the left, using the

short left–long right principle but in an extended lunging attitude, rather like a fencer, into the ...
4. **Hitting area** just behind the shuttle which is now at full arm's stretch away then ...
5. **Hit** the shuttle in the manner described under each shot description below, then ...
6. **Follow after** the shuttle along the trajectory of, and at the pace of, the particular shot selected to finally ...
7. **Recover** to position of readiness by moving the feet in reverse order to the outgoing travel element.

Particular note: aim to reach all of these shots with just *one* bounce, *one* short and *one* long step. No more should be needed!

Drives – Forehand and Backhand – Wide of the Body

OBJECTIVE – DRIVES
These should be taken at, or slightly above, shoulder level. Aim to hit the shuttle hard with a fast flat trajectory to pass just

45

above the net wide of the opponent, to fall into his mid-court area.

OBJECTIVE – BLOCK RETURNS

Taken at shoulder height or any point below this down to floor level. To gently direct the shuttle up and over the net to fall down into the opponent's forecourt area.

OBJECTIVE – HIGH LIFTS

Taken at shoulder height or any point below this down to floor level. To hit the shuttle, again quickly, but with an upwards trajectory which takes the shuttle above the maximum upwards reach of the opponent and into his back court areas.

All these shots are used constantly within the doubles game, particularly mixed doubles; also block returns to, and high lifts from, smashes in singles.

FOREHAND DRIVES
(Figs 51–4)

Point of impact is in front of and wide of the body. The racket is held with a loose forehand grip, racket arm bent with elbow at shoulder level, racket hand close to the right ear to bring the racket behind the head, right shoulder pulled back as far as possible. Hit the shuttle by throwing the right shoulder forward, followed by vigorous arm throwing. As the arm straightens to strike the shuttle at full arm's stretch, uncock the hand and tighten the fingers sharply for fast racket head speed. Maintain momentum with a strong follow-after in the intended direction of the shot then let the racket hand 'recover' to the front of the body.

BACKHAND DRIVES
(Figs 55–8)

Point of impact is in front of and wide of the body. The racket is held with a loose backhand grip, racket arm bent with elbow at shoulder level, racket hand close to the left ear to bring the racket behind the head, right shoulder back as far as possible, most of the back towards the net. Strike the shuttle by throwing the right shoulder towards the net, followed by vigorous arm throwing. As the arm straightens, enabling the shuttle to be struck at full arm's stretch, uncock the hand and tighten the fingers quickly to produce very rapid racket head speed. If executed correctly, the shoulder and elbow joints will 'lock', therefore follow-after is virtually non-existent. It is essential to ensure that at moment of impact the racket face is presented precisely at right angles to the intended path and trajectory of the shot.

SIMPLE PRACTICES

Before hitting shuttles practise, by 'shadowing', all of the movements for the two shots described above, first as individual shots then by linking them together as a preliminary warm-up.

From position of readiness: bounce – travel to forehand – hit – recover to position of readiness. From position of readiness: bounce – turn and travel to backhand – hit – recover to position of readiness.

For actual hitting practice, prepare in the position of readiness astride the centre line, towards the back of your mid-court area. Feeding for these shots is probably best achieved by having shuttles thrown. Have your 'feed' throw a shuttle towards the inner side boundary line just in front of your forehand reach and at shoulder level. Make sure he is not in line with your hard-hit shots! Remember that you must take the shuttle at full arm's stretch. Practise all of the elements for the flat drive: bounce,

46

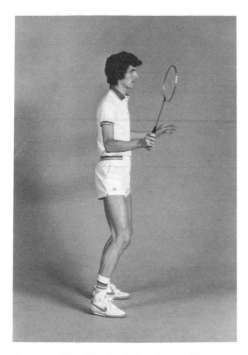

Fig 51   Shoulder high forehand drive –
preparation. Position of readiness prior to
lunging into striking atittude.

Fig 52   Striking attitude. Extended lunge,
elbow at height of intended hitting and
racket behind head.

Fig 53   Hitting. Hand has been uncocked
at end of arm throwing, point of impact
slightly in front of body.

Fig 54   Racket and arm follow-after.
Follow after in direction of shot played and
then across front of body.

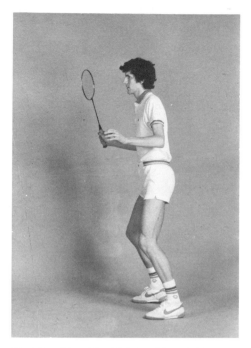

Fig 55   Shoulder high backhand drive –
preparation. Position of readiness prior to
lunging into striking attitude.

Fig 56   Striking attitude. Extended
lunge, elbow at height of intended hitting
and racket behind head.

Fig 57   Hitting. Hand has been uncocked
at end of arm straightening, point of impact
slightly in front of body.

Fig 58   Racket and arm follow-after.
Follow after in direction of shot played with
wrist action only.

short left step, long right lunge into the hitting position. Hit the shuttle fast, flat and straight over the net. Recover to position of readiness. Repeat this a number of times, always ensuring that the entire stroke cycle is completed between each shot.

Next, practise in exactly the same manner but with the shuttle being fed down the backhand side of the court. Again ensure that the complete stroke cycle is completed between each shot.

ADJUSTMENTS

Shuttles leave the racket on both sides of the body, with very sharp impact sounds, travel straight, flat and fast, just skimming the top of the net to fall in the opponent's mid-court. Change nothing but continue practising, both forehand and backhand drives, until the actions become 'grooved'.

Shuttle hits the net Have you hit the shuttle at the correct height – shoulder level? Are you keeping the racket head vertical at point of impact or is it turning, introducing a degree of 'top slice'? Is follow-after being maintained in the intended direction of the shots?

Shuttle has an upwards trajectory Is the shuttle being allowed to fall below shoulder level? Point of impact should be at, or just above, shoulder level. Is the racket head vertical at point of impact? Or has your grip changed slightly, introducing an element of 'bottom slice'? Is follow-after in the intended direction of the shot? See notes regarding variations.

Shuttles travel in wrong direction Check the impact points. Are you hitting the shuttle too early, sending it cross-court, or too late, sending it out of court? The cross-court shot

is dealt with later, the out of court shot is obviously unacceptable. At this stage make the necessary correction to drive the shuttle straight.

Shuttles have a looped trajectory and fall short Check the impact point again – are you too near to the shuttle, not taking the shuttle at full arm's stretch? Is the uncocking action powerful enough? See notes regarding variations.

VARIATIONS

Flat drive played cross-court Still take the shuttle at, or slightly above shoulder height, but change the impact point so that it is slightly further in front of the body. Follow-after will be positively in the intended direction of the shot.

Flat block return The objective is to play gently into the opponent's forecourt. This shot is basically the equivalent of a 'drop' but off the drive action. As with the overhead drops, the aim is to disguise your intentions to deceive the opponent into believing that a powerful drive is being played. Without changing any part of your prep-aration, movement and arm action, *immediately* prior to striking you must slow the hand action dramatically. Follow-after should continue exactly as for the usual drive action to maintain the illusion for as long as possible. Shuttles should leave the racket gently to travel just over the top of, and then fall down close to, the net. These shots can be played both straight and cross-court with point of impact changes as for flat drives.

Practise by having your feed throw the shuttles to you as before but now hit not beyond him but back into his hands. The intention is to develop skills which produce soft returns off what must appear to the opponent to be hard-hitting techniques. As with the overhead shots practise the art of disguise and deception.

Flat high lift This can best be considered as a shoulder high drive but *up* and over the opponent to the very back of his court. It can be achieved simply by effecting a slight alteration of the racket face angle to the shuttle and ensuring that follow-after is powerfully in the intended direction.

Drive actions from below shoulder level The second of our objectives related to shuttles taken below shoulder level of which there are only two to consider: block returns and high lifts. But for one slight change they are played with exactly the same stroke cycle as for the drives but to counter shots which have been directed *down* into the mid-court area. The only change is that the elbow points down at the intended point of impact rather than staying at shoulder level. For the bigger shot follow-after will be into, through and then up in the intended direction of the shot. If taken very low, this upwards trajectory will have to be steep to clear the net and the maximum reach of the opponent with the intention of reaching the back of the court. Obviously, the shuttle can be taken earlier, therefore higher, and played with a flatter trajectory. In these cases, care must be taken to ensure that the shuttle clears the maximum reach of the opponent and, very importantly, is not over-hit to fall out of court.

SIMPLE PRACTICES
Practices should be precisely the same as for the flat drives but in both cases with your feed throwing shuttles from the net in order to achieve the necessary downwards trajectory to which you have to respond. Again practise forehand and backhand shots, straight and cross-court. Remember that throughout these practices you should emphasise both the elbow pointing and follow-after elements of the stroke making, which make these shots different from the flat drives.

Shots to be practised will be:

Underarm high lifts struck very hard with a trajectory which clears the opponent's maximum upwards reach to fall into his back court. Practise both straight and cross-court shots off both forehand and backhand.

Underarm block returns with an upwards trajectory, hit gently to pass close to and just over the net, and from there to fall straight down into the oppponent's forecourt. Practise both straight and cross-court versions of this shot. As you become more and more competent you can start to introduce disguise and deception.

UNDERARM SHOTS
(Fig 59)

Previous sections have covered shots from the back and mid-courts leaving only those for the forecourt. These come under two general headings, the first of which is the Underarm; the stroke cycle for this is as follows.

1. **Prepare**, with a small bounce on the balls of the toes, and adopt the appropriate ...
2. **Stroke striking attitude**, either under-

arm forehand or backhand striking attitude appropriate to the shot to be played.

3. **Travel**, racket foot striking, i.e., right foot always in advance of the left, using the short left–long right principle but in an extended lunging attitude, rather like a fencer, into the ...

4. **Hitting area** just behind the shuttle which is now at full arm's stretch away then ...

5. **Hit** the shuttle in the manner described under each shot description which follows, then ...

6. **Follow after** the shuttle along the trajectory of, and at the pace of, the particular shot selected finally to ...

7. **Recover** to position of readiness by moving the feet in reverse order to the outgoing travel element.

Particular note: aim to reach all of these shots with just *one* bounce, *one* short step and *one* long lunge. No more should be needed.

Lifts – Forehand and Backhand

OBJECTIVE

To hit the shuttle from as near the top of the net as possible, and hit it to the back of the court with a steep upwards trajectory, well above the maximum reach of the opponent; ideally to fall vertically down into the very back of the opponent's back court. The shot is used frequently within the singles game; less so in doubles.

FOREHAND LIFT
(Figs 60–63)

The shot striking attitude is virtually identical to that for the drive actions except that the movements are forwards rather than sideways. Move to the hitting area with a bounce, short and long step. Point of impact will be in front and/or wide of the body. The racket is held with a loose forehand grip, arm bent so that the elbow is below the hand, hand cocked back so that the racket head is below the hand. Hit the

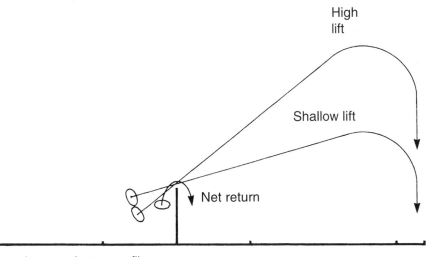

Fig 59   Underarm shots – trajectory profiles.

Fig 60   Underarm forehand lift –
preparation. Position of readiness prior to
moving to take shuttle.

Fig 61   Striking attitude. Extended lunge,
arm slightly bent with elbow down prior to
straightening and hand cocked.

Fig 62   Hitting. Arm straightened and
hand uncocked.

Fig 63   Follow-after. Extended straight
arm following after in direction of shot.

shuttle by first straightening the arm to reach the impact point and then uncocking the hand while quickly tightening the fingers. Ensure that the hand does *not* uncock beyond point of impact. Shot momentum is maintained, primarily, by following after the intended direction of the shot with the extended arm. The shot will have been played off an extended racket foot. Do not let the non-racket foot move from the extended lunge, but, having played the shot, take weight back onto it and recover to position of readiness.

BACKHAND LIFT
(Figs 64–7)
Point of impact will be in front and/or wide of the body. The racket is held with a loose backhand grip, arm bent with elbow at shoulder level, the racket hand below the elbow, the hand cocked back so that the racket is below the hand. The racket head should be close to the left hip. Some part of the back will be turned to the net. Hit the shuttle by first straightening the arm to reach into the hitting area and then quickly both uncocking the hand and tightening the fingers. Put impact snap into the hitting by projecting 'weight' through the thumb and ensuring the hand does not uncock beyond point of impact. If executed correctly, both shoulder and elbow joints will have 'locked', therefore follow-after is limited to the racket head only, in the intended direction of the shot. The shot is played off an extended racket foot. Do not let the non-racket foot move from the extended lunge but, having played the shot, take weight back onto it and recover to position of readiness.

SIMPLE PRACTICES
Stand, in the position of readiness astride the centre line, in about the mid-court position. Have the feed, standing close to the net, throw shuttles gently up and over the net so that they fall close to and steeply down your side of the net – see the net shot trajectory. First, have the shuttle fed just wide of the centre line on your forehand side so that you do not have too far to reach. Progressively the shuttles should be fed wider thus increasing the distance over which you must lunge and stretch. Remember that you wish to take the shuttle at full arm's stretch, and preferably at shoulder level. Practise all of the elements of the lift, i.e., short left step, long lunge with racket foot and hit the shuttle quickly and steeply upwards to reach the back of the court. Recover to position of readiness. Next, practise in precisely the same manner, but with the shuttle being fed down the backhand side of the court.

ADJUSTMENTS
Shuttles leave the racket, on both sides of the body, with sharp impact sounds, travel fast, straight and high to fall close to the back boundary line. Change nothing but continue practising both forehand and backhand lifts, until both these actions become grooved.

Shuttles travel high but fall short, i.e. fail to reach the back line Did you take the shuttle at the top of the net or from a much lower level? Have you kept the momentum (follow-after) going sufficiently? Was the arm straightened quickly and the hand uncocked vigorously? Were you at full arm's stretch or too close to the shuttles?

Shuttles do not reach a great height and also fall short See comments above.

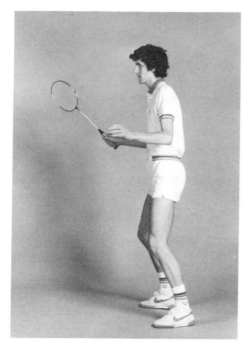

Fig 64   Underarm backhand lift –
preparation. Position of readiness prior to
moving to take the shuttle.

Fig 65   Striking attitude. Extended lunge,
arm fully bent prior to straightening and
hand cocked.

Fig 66   Hitting. Arm straightened and
hand uncocked.

Fig 67   Follow-after. Extended straight
arm following after in direction of shot.

Shuttles travel in the wrong direction
Check your impact points. Are you hitting the shuttle too early, sending it cross-court, or too late, sending it out of court? The cross-court shot is dealt with later; the out of court shot is obviously unacceptable. At this stage make the necessary corrections to lift the shuttles straight.

VARIATIONS
High lifts played cross-court Still taking the shuttle precisely as directed earlier, change the impact points so that these are slightly further in front of the body. The racket face will be at a slightly different· angle as a result. Follow-after momentum is in the intended direction of the shots.

Lifts with flatter trajectories Ideally the shuttles should be taken even higher in front of you than for the usual lift. You will need to be very fast moving to achieve this! Alternatively, the shuttles may be taken later, consequently lower and further away from the net in order to obtain the correct trajectory. Otherwise all of the elements of hitting remain unchanged. It is essential that these shots are above the maximum upwards reach of the opponent. Cross-court flat lifts must be used only with discretion – they can all too easily be cut off by the opponent.

Straight net returns These are basically the equivalent of 'drops' played off the high lift action. That is, they travel up and over the net to fall into the opponent's forecourt area. As with all of the drops described previously, the aim is to disguise your intentions and deceive the opponent into believing that a powerful shot is about to be played. Therefore, no part of the very dynamic preparation, travel and hitting

movements required for the lifts must be changed. Instead, *immediately* prior to hitting the arm is straightened vigorously but the hand is slowed dramatically, or not uncocked at all, to bring the racket head to a standstill. The shuttle is allowed to 'bounce' off the racket to travel gently up and over and then fall down very close to the net. To practise the shots, proceed exactly as described for the lifts, with the feed throwing shuttles gently up and over the net. Practise all of the elements of the shot, i.e., short left step, long lunge with racket foot and 'hit the shuttle' (in reality simply let it bounce off a stationary racket) to bounce up and over the net back to the feed. Recover to position of readiness. Next, practise in precisely the same manner, but with the shuttle being fed down the backhand side of the court.

Angled net shots

Like all of the other shots underarm net shots can also be played across the court, i.e, directed away from the point at which they are taken. Note the use of the word 'directed' rather than 'hit'.

OBJECTIVE
To convince the opponent that a straight shot from the net is to be played, then to angle the shuttle away from him by sending it along the net to fall in his forecourt. This shot is used extensively in all forms of the game.

METHOD
Proceed precisely as described for straight net returns. The entire stroke cycle remains unchanged up to point of hitting. The racket head is flat (parallel to the floor) as the arm is straightened, until immediately before

impact at which point the loosely held racket is manipulated with the fingers to alter the angle of the racket head slightly. The outside edge of the racket head is turned upwards and moved gently in the direction of the shot being played. Think in terms of rolling the racket head. To send the shuttle from right to left roll the racket anti-clockwise; from 9–3 o'clock to 8–2 o'clock. Roll clockwise from 9–3 o'clock to 10–4 o'clock to send the shuttle from left to right. Like all finger touch shots these will require lots of practice.

SIMPLE PRACTICE

This will be precisely as described for the straight net returns. Remember the objective is to incorporate disguise and deception when the shots are played. Turning the racket head must be delayed until the very last moment. Do you send the shuttle away from the feed to the other side of court? Did he think you were about to play the straight shot?

HITTING DOWN FROM THE NET
(Figs 68 & 69)

OBJECTIVE

To hit the shuttle quickly and steeply down from the net in your forecourt either to beat the opponent completely or draw weak lifted responses. The shots are used extensively in all forms of games play.

METHOD

These shots should not be confused with the smashes, either forehand or backhand, played from further back in the court. Hitting down from the net shots are played following a forward step and lunge, as for the other net shots. In this case the elbow is down and the racket head is above the hand to deliver a short, sharp tap to the shuttle. The tap action is very important, because firstly the limited follow-after for this hitting action helps to avoid striking the net with the racket, which could be a fault; secondly, because it is impossible to 'wind-up' for a powerful smash if the body is at full stretch forwards – which it should be.

The more outstretched the body the greater the difficulty of sharply 'tapping' down. The shots are likely to fall into the mid, even back, courts, to still, nonetheless, be winners. If you are fast enough commit yourself totally to the 'kill'. Leap lunge forward allowing the back foot to come close to the racket foot before thinking about a recovery. After all if you win the rally you do not need to recover quickly!

Shots can be played with either the forehand or backhand hitting actions. In both cases make sure that the hand is cocked back, you have a loose grip on the racket and that the arm is bent. As you move quickly forward with upraised racket, reach out by straightening the arm, uncock the hand and quickly tighten the grip. Remember that you require a short, sharp tapping action. Do not follow after. Slight modifications to the grip may be necessary to ensure that the racket head hits the shuttle in the intended direction.

SIMPLE PRACTICES

Commence by assuming that you have completed the movements to the shot and have reached a point close to the net. The arm is bent, elbow down to bring the racket head closer to the face, racket held loosely with adjusted grip so that the racket face is in the intended direction of your shot. Your feed can practise his low serve towards your racket, but aiming some six inches

Fig 68　Forehand striking down at the net – preparation. Body almost erect with left foot brought close to right, arm bent with elbow down, racket head up.

Fig 69　Striking. Arm straightened quickly to strike shuttle downwards.

above the top of the net, or could throw shuttles up with an under-hand action. Practise hitting the shuttle down sharply, taking care to direct it away from the feed. Both forehand and backhand shots must be practised. Now move further away from the hitting position and practise again; one step forward and hit. Progressively start from further back in the court until, eventually, you can complete the entire stroke cycle.

You should also practise the 'dead racket' variation of this shot, namely, with a threatening leap forward simply allow the shuttle to bounce off the upraised racket and fall gently down close to the net.

Practise tapping sharply straight, to the left and to the right with both backhand and forehand grips to learn the slightly different holds on the racket.

ADJUSTMENTS

Shuttles leave the racket with sharp tapping sounds, whether from immediately in front, to the left or to the right of the body, to pass quickly over the net and down into the opponent's mid-court. Change nothing but continue the practice and do not be satisfied until all of the actions are totally grooved.

Shuttles are sharply 'tapped' but hit the net Have you leapt/reached far enough forward? Is the head of the racket sufficiently raised? You must meet the shuttle while it is still rising and can clear the net on its way back after your shot.

Shuttles are sharply 'tapped' but travel out of the back of the opponent's court
Have you pushed the racket forward rather than tapping down? Have you arrived at point of impact late, consequently being too far back to do more than hit from below net tape level with a flat rather than downwards trajectory?

While you will correct as many faults as possible always bear in mind that these types of shot have an in-built 'degree of difficulty'. They are short, sharp touch shots delivered at the end of very rapid forward movements. They also require a great deal of energy if executed correctly. Therefore practise them little but often: the recipe for dedicated, high-quality practice.

SUMMARY

This completes the chapter on basic shot making. Ensure that you practise all of the shots constantly in order that they become grooved to the point that you can play them instinctively. Equally ensure that they are practised in their entirety. Badminton is as much about the feet as the fist. Unless the feet are practised in moving the body both efficiently and effectively the hitting techniques will be compromised.

By this stage you will have acquired sufficient skills to advance from casual games play to enter into rather more serious game competition.

4
Playing the Game

At the outset it was stated that for the beginner, practices should be a balanced mixture of games play and specific stroke and shot practices. The basic stroke and shot making techniques have now been covered in detail. Whilst practising these skills you should also engage in games play even if this is only at the most elementary of levels. To assist you in this there follows a simplified explanation of the rules of the game.

RULES

Areas of play, as defined by the Laws of Badminton, are shown in the diagrams. (As the Laws are revised from time to time it is recommended that the reader ensures that he is fully aware of the latest interpretation of these). Courts are usually marked out to cover both doubles and singles areas. The diagrams illustrate the different areas for both types of game. Consider these in conjunction with the following explanations.

Area of Play

LEVEL AND MIXED DOUBLES
(Fig 70)
The entire marked area is to be used once the shuttle has been served and a rally is in progress. You ignore the inner line markings both at the sides and back of the

court. When serving, the shuttle must fall in the diagonally opposite serving/receiving area. This area extends from the centre line to the outermost side boundary line and from the front service line to the inner back boundary line. Again you ignore the inner side markings. But, should the shuttle fall beyond the back inner boundary line when serving, it is considered 'out', and is therefore a fault.

SINGLES
(Fig 71)
This game is played within the confines of the inner side-lines and the outer back boundary line. That is, you ignore the outer side boundary lines. A shuttle falling outside the inner side-lines is 'out', and is therefore a fault. When serving, the shuttle must fall within the diagonally opposite serving/receiving area. This area extends from the centre line to the innermost side boundary line and from the front service line to the outer back boundary line. The inner back boundary line is ignored.

Playing – General

DOUBLES
The game is played between four players, two on each side of the net, and is started by one player serving the shuttle. Serves are strictly governed by the Laws (see Chapter 2) and the first of these must be

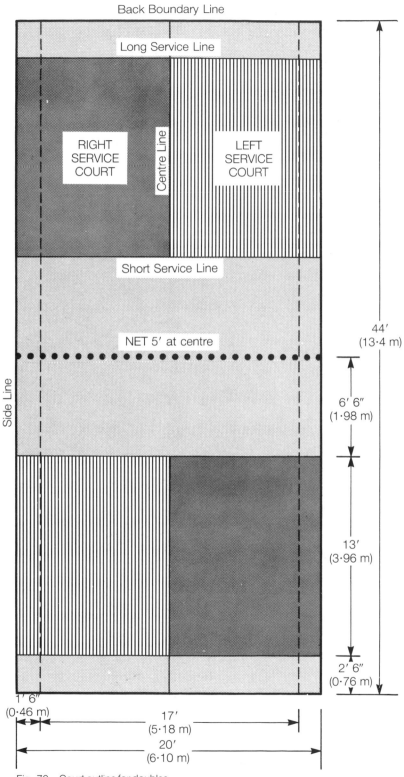

Back Boundary Line

Long Service Line

RIGHT SERVICE COURT

Centre Line

LEFT SERVICE COURT

Short Service Line

NET 5' at centre

Side Line

44'
(13·4 m)

6' 6"
(1·98 m)

13'
(3·96 m)

2' 6"
(0·76 m)

1' 6"
(0·46 m)

17'
(5·18 m)

20'
(6·10 m)

Fig 70   Court outline for doubles.

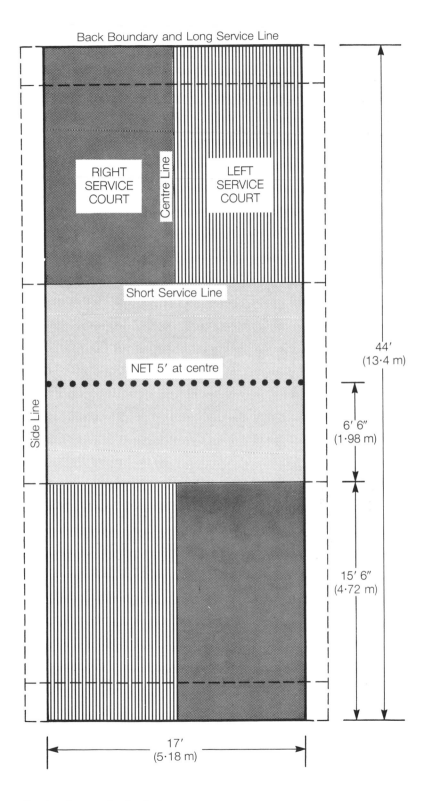

Fig 71   Court outline for singles.

from the right-hand court over and diagonally across the net to the receiver's right-hand court. Only the receiver may return this service but thereafter any player can hit the shuttle to maintain a rally. The rally continues in a series of volleys (the shuttle must not be allowed to strike the floor) and the shuttle must pass over the net. A rally is lost when one of the pairs fails to hit the shuttle over the net, hits the shuttle outside the outer boundary lines, allows the shuttle to fall to the fall or contravenes one of the Laws.

SINGLES

The game is played between two players and is started by one player serving the shuttle. Whilst some of the serves may be different to those employed in doubles they are, equally, governed by the Laws of Badminton. Again the first service must be from the right-hand court, the shuttle being hit over and diagonally across the net to the receiver's right-hand court. Thereafter the rally continues exactly as for doubles and is terminated in the same manner. Essentially, the only difference is that it is played within the confines of the narrower singles court area.

Scoring

You can only score points when you (or your partner in doubles) are serving.

In all forms of men's, ladies' and mixed doubles, and also men's singles, play the side that first scores fifteen points wins a game. Games in ladies' singles are won by the player that first scores eleven points.

However, 'setting' is allowed in all forms of games play. Before August 1998 this was relatively complicated, but is now greatly simplified. The result of the new ruling is to limit the number of 'setting' points to three in any form of games play as follows.

In ladies' singles the setting option arises when the score reaches ten-all. The lady first reaching that score then has the option of either continuing the game to eleven points or 'setting' to three. That is, continuing the game until one or other of the players reaches thirteen first.

Setting for men's, ladies' and mixed doubles and men's singles play is permitted when the score reaches fourteen-all. The side first reaching fourteen has the option of either continuing the game to fifteen points or 'setting' to three. The game will either finish at 15–14 or when one of the sides first reaches seventeen.

Particularly note that there is no obligation upon the side first reaching 'set' point to 'set'. However, as the service is with their opponent(s) when a decision has to be made they would be unwise to select this option. Therefore this latest ruling almost certainly guarantees that all 'set' games will be continued for another three points.

Usually a match comprises three games. Players change ends at the commencement of the second game and again for the third game. In the third game, the players again change ends when the leading score is eight points when playing doubles and men's singles, or six points when playing ladies' singles.

HOW TO SCORE

First toss to determine who has first choice of the following options. The winning side has the option of serving first (in which case the other side must choose an end), not serving first (in which case the other side must decide between serving first or choosing an end) or choosing an end (in which case the other side must serve first).

In the singles game the server, serving first from the right-hand court, scores a point if he wins the rally. He then serves from the left-hand court and, provided he wins that rally, adds another point to his score, serves again from the right-hand court, and so on. When he loses a rally the serve passes to his opponent who then has to win a rally to score.

For doubles the serving and scoring arrangements are basically the same, except that all players have to serve in turn. However, there is a slight complication for the pair that serves first. When starting the game, the pair electing to serve first starts 'one hand down', that is, they have only one player entitled to serve. That player serves first from the right-hand court to one opponent. If that rally is won, a point is gained and that same player serves again but from the left-hand court to the second opponent. The game continues until the serving side loses a rally at which point the service passes to the opponents. This situation occurs only once – at the beginning of each game. The pair having just lost the right to serve must receive from the service sides of their court from which the last service was played until such time as they regain the right to serve. For example, if the score at time of losing the right to serve was even (0, 2, 4, and so on) the original server will receive and next serve from the right-hand court. If the number of points scored is uneven (1, 3, 5, and so on) then the original server will receive and next serve from the left-hand court.

The service is now with the opponents and the player on the right-hand side of the court serves first. He continues serving, first from the right-hand court and then the left, scoring points as each rally is won by his side, until a rally is lost. His partner then serves from the right or left-hand side of the court, depending upon whether the score is even or odd. Again he serves first from one side and then the other until his side loses the rally when the right to serve passes back to the original servers. The player in the right-hand court, either the original first server or his partner depending upon the score, serves until a rally is lost. Now his partner serves until a rally is lost. Once that pair have both lost the serve the service passes back to their opponents and so on. Remember that the players move from one side of the court to the other only whilst they are serving. Once they have lost the serve they must remain on the same side from which they last served but only to receive serves from their opponents. During rallies all the players may move to any part of the court they choose or that is dictated to them by the opponents' shots.

The explanations of the different games and the scoring for these have been reduced to their simplest elements. In addition to the Laws governing the service action, already explained in detail, there are a number of other laws which must be observed. The more important of these are listed below. When considering these it is important to realise that they are those ruling at time of writing. As the Laws are revised from time to time it is essential that you are in possession, and fully aware, of the current Laws. They can be obtained from the International Badminton Federation or your national governing body.

Service Faults

The current Laws relating to serves are outlined in Chapter 2. It is also a fault:

1. If the feet of the player receiving the service are not in the service/receiving court diagonally opposite until the service is delivered.

2. If, once the service has started, any player makes preliminary feints or otherwise intentionally baulks his opponent.

3. If, either in service or play, the shuttle falls outside the boundaries of the court, or passes through or under the net, or fails to pass the net, or touches the roof or side walls, or the person or dress of a player. (A shuttle falling on a line shall be deemed to have fallen in the court or service court of which such line is a boundary.)

4. If, when in play, the initial contact with the shuttle is not on the striker's side of the net. (The striker may, however, follow the shuttle over the net with his racket in the course of a stroke.)

5. If, when the shuttle is in play, a player touches the net or its supports with racket, person or dress.

6. If the shuttle be caught and held on the racket and then slung during the execution of a stroke; or if the shuttle be hit twice in succession by the same player with two strokes; or if the shuttle be hit by a player and his partner successively.

7. If, in play, a player strikes the shuttle (unless he thereby makes a good return) or is struck by it, whether he is within or outside the boundaries of the court.

8. If a player obstructs an opponent.

9. If the server serves before his opponent is ready, but the opponent shall be deemed to be ready if a return is attempted.

10. If the receiver moves before the service is delivered (hit by the server).

Initially it is not too important to observe all of the Laws, but to endeavour to start to enjoy rallying within the game situation. Obviously, as you develop your ability to play the game, so the Laws play a more important role.

GAMES PLAY

Now we can consider in more detail how each of the three different forms of the game should be played, that is, the tactics to be employed. Essentially, tactics are logical solutions to situations which are actu-ally encountered in games play. In addition to allowing you to exploit your opponent's deficiencies in technique, fitness and tactical application, tactics should also have regard to protecting your own side from the opponent's attempts to exploit any weakness it may have. The advice in the following pages makes a number of dogmatic statements to try to establish 'basic' tactics. Whilst these dogmas remain valid at all levels of play, it must be realised that they are subject to adaptation and/or modification dependent upon individuals and circumstances.

Each of the three different forms of games play is covered by comment under the following six headings; Serving, Receiving Serves, Attacking Shots, Defensive Shots and Basing (Positional Considerations). The subject headings are supplemented by diagrams.

Notes

1. As always, all descriptions of forehand and backhand shots and situations assume one or two right-handed players.

2. Under the Singles heading court areas to which different shots should be hit are boldly highlighted. The same shots in other games and situations should be directed to the same court areas.

Singles

Essential requirements are fitness, a complete repertoire of shots and a particular feeling for the game, the latter acquired from regular practice. The shape of the singles court is long and narrow which, to a certain extent, dictates the manner in which the game is played.

SERVING
(Fig 72)
High serves should be in the majority, from within the server's base and directed to the extreme boundary of the back court. Most will be towards the centre, rather than outer, boundary line. High serves ensure that the receiver has to move well away from his base and play his returns over the maximum distance of the court. They allow you more time to prepare for his responses and, by serving down the middle, also reduce the angle of his returns. From time to time high serves should be directed towards the side-lines, particularly if these exploit a weakness in the receiver's responses. Low serves into the opponent's forecourt should not be neglected, indeed, at the very highest levels they are used extensively but you must be very fit to employ them in this way. They can be used, with discretion, if the receiver stands too far back, and/or has a limited repertoire of net returns. Again, a quickly hit low trajectory high or drive serve to the back of the opponent's mid-court may unsettle him to draw a poor response.

RECEIVING SERVES
(Fig 73)
Firstly ensure that your receiving stance is adopted within your 'base'. This base should be neither too far forward, thus leaving you open to the 'flicked' serve, or too far back, allowing the server to draw a poor lifted return if he serves low. It should be closer to the centre than the side-line. The receiving attitude should be 'expectant', non-racket foot forward and racket up, allowing you to move quickly either backwards or forwards to take the shuttle, once served, at its highest point. Concentrate your attention on the server and his serving action as you have only milliseconds to respond to his serve. The 'loose' serve, that is a shallow trajectory high serve falling short or a low serve which is high above the net, should be dealt with severely by smashing or striking down at the net into the mid-court. Good high serves can be played in a number of ways – see Attacking Shots below. The good low serve should be returned as a tight net return into the forecourt, best played away from the server, or pushed flat and fast away from the server and into the mid or back courts. If you are obliged to lift ensure that this is very high and reaches the very extremes of the back court.

ATTACKING SHOTS
Your objective is to ensure that the opponent covers the maximum area of his court in responding to your shots, whilst minimising your movements. All shots are played with the principle of attack as their basis provided they are well directed – poorly directed shots provide the opponent with attacking opportunities.

A large proportion of your shots will be clears, ideally forehand but if necessary off the backhand, to force your opponent to play his shots from the extremes of his back court areas. Occasionally, when sufficiently well positioned and with the opponent well forward, you can use flat

Fig 72   Poul-Erik Hoyer-Larsen of Denmark just on the point of high serving. Note position close to centre line, hand starting to uncock as the shuttle is released and weight now transferred onto the racket foot.

Fig 73   Poul-Erik Hoyer-Larsen again but now about to receive his opponent's serve. Attentive and with legs flexed prepared to spring into action the moment the serve is delivered.

67

attacking clears to catch him unawares and place him under even greater pressure to cover the back of the court. Clears will be played both straight and cross-court, always well directed so that the opponent has to move away from his base. Often clears directed to the same area in quick succession can upset the opponent's ability to respond positively, particularly when shots are aimed at his backhand.

Smashes will be employed when the shuttle is falling short of your back line and you have been able to get behind it. Direct these steeply down into the mid-court areas. They will mostly be directed away from the opponent, calling for both straight and cross-court smashes, but playing them straight at his body may produce dividends. Do not assume that these will bring immediate winners but anticipate a weak lifted return and be prepared to punish this further.

Drops, off either clear or smash actions, will be used to achieve the same results as smashes – either outright winners or poor responses from the opponent. They must, of course, be directed to fall into the opponent's forecourt areas. Remember the need for deception: the opponent will anticipate other shots if you successfully disguise your intentions. Again, they must be played both straight and cross-court on both forehand and backhand strokes. Drops to the middle of the net can be introduced to good effect, allowing you to base centrally and reduce angles of returns.

Net shots into the forecourt are an important element of your attacking game. Played tightly to the net, either straight or along the net, they can produce outright winners or oblige your opponent to play another net shot allowing you to hit the shuttle down; or allow him only to lift the shuttle to mid-court giving you the opportunity of an easy kill.

DEFENSIVE SHOTS

Your opponent will have precisely the same objectives as you, that is to be constantly on the attack by employing the shots described above. It is essential that your defending abilities are equal to his attacking game.

Clears are an important part in our defensive armour. The very high clear when under pressure will enable you both to stay in a rally and recover to a base.

The ability to return smashes must be developed so that not only can it be used defensively but also to turn defence into attack. You must develop an ability to play underarm retrieving shots in a variety of ways: to drive the shuttle back over and close to the top of the net, thus preventing your opponent from playing the second smash; more gently so that it passes close to the top of, then steeply down the net, forcing him to move quickly forward only to take the shuttle below tape level; or by lifting powerfully and steeply upwards to pass over the advancing opponent and fall near the back boundary line.

Returns to your opponent's drops must be taken as early as possible – your speed of forward movement is an extremely important factor in both defence and attack – to play either a sharply struck net kill or a tight net return. Alternatively, you may elect to lift the shuttle steeply upwards towards the back boundary line.

As when attacking, your defensive shots should aim to move your opponent away from his base and, more particularly, oblige him to change his direction of movement completely as often as possible. You must also develop the ability to play all of these returns off both forehand and backhand sides of the body.

BASING
(Fig 74)

In very general terms your 'base' will be an area in the centre of your court, i.e. equidistant from the extreme corners, the precise position and size of which will be determined by experience. It may also have to be influenced by your repertoire of shots, if, for example, a lack of adequate backhand shots means you have to protect these from the opponent's attacks. Recovery to this base should be made between each shot played. Ideally, you should reach this base before the shuttle reaches the opponent's racket, to allow maximum time for 'reading', and then responding to, your opponent's next shot.

As your ability to play the singles game improves you can introduce elements of 'bias basing' both to reduce your next movements and narrow the angles of the opponent's returns.

1. After shots to the opponent's forecourt areas quickly recover to the front of your base area.

2. After shots to the opponent's forehand mid and rear court areas quickly recover to the left side of your base area.

3. After shots to the opponent's backhand mid and rear court areas quickly recover to the right side of your base.

Level Doubles

Level doubles describes both men's and the ladies' doubles games. Usually ladies cannot play the most powerful shots of the game as strongly or for as long as the men. However, at higher levels of competitive play, while the ladies may lack the power they do not lack the energy or variety of shot and certainly not the subtlety which is so important in the doubles games. As we must all aspire to achieve this highest level, the following narrative is directed to that end and we will, therefore, consider the two games as one. Once again, essential ingredients are fitness, a complete repertoire of shots and, most particularly, as a result of constantly playing together, the ability of the pair to 'think as one'.

The court areas are now wider but, of course, covered by two players, dictating the need to consider how they best deploy themselves in particular situations. This is covered in greater detail under Triangular Bases. For the time being it is sufficient to know that we have a front and back player when attacking, while the defensive formation requires the players to be alongside one another.

SERVING
(Fig 75)

Serving is the means of starting a rally within the games situation. The Laws allow us to score points only when serving. It is imperative, therefore, that the serving side starts the rally in a manner which enables it to draw from the receivers a response which is more to the serving side's advantage than the reverse. At higher levels of badminton play 'aces' are notably absent!

In doubles, serving should be conducted in concert with your partner. Do not serve before your partner is prepared, like you, to launch immediately into an attack once the serve is delivered (hit). The server's partner must adopt a 'position of immediate readiness' close behind the server, a position that still permits a full view of the opponent

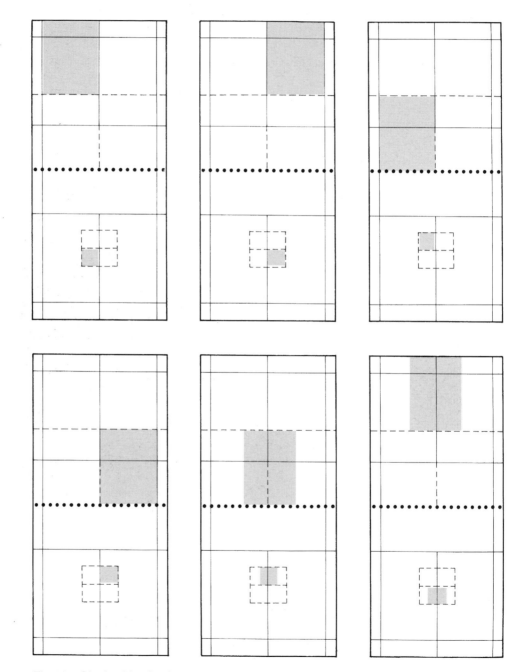

Fig 74   Singles bias basing position – the basic principles of bias between shots.

Fig 75   Par Gunnar Jonson and Peter Axelson, both of Sweden. Every aspect of Par's serving complies with the Laws. Note both Par's concentration on his task and Peter's on the oncoming responses of their opponents.

and their court area, but that also allows immediate responses to returns to the serves.

Low serves will be in the majority and are played from an attacking formation, mostly directed towards the centre of the opponents' front service line. The softer returns to the net to be dealt with sharply by the quickly following-in server with net kills or tight net returns. If the receiver opts to lift the shuttle into mid or back court the server's partner moves quickly to hit smashes or fast, not slow, drops. Only in the most exceptional of circumstances will the serving side abdicate from the attacking role and play other than these shots. Very seldom are games won by low serves alone, therefore early in the game the servers should determine the responses of their opponents to flick and drive serves.

Flick and drive serves, played with disguise and deception may not obtain outright winners but could have the effect of drawing loose returns from the receiver. They will also stop your opponents too often attacking your low serves as they become accustomed to the predictability of these. Essentially these serves are of an attacking nature *but* they permit the receiver to hit down! Therefore, immediately either type of serve is delivered the serving pair must move into the side-by-side defensive formation! The receiver's drops are met with tight net returns or net kills; smashes with tight net block returns or high lifts; clears with smashes or drops. If all else fails your side resorts to high serves.

High serves must be to the very back of the receiving court area to give your side time to move to the side-by-side defensive formation. You have given away the attack and must now rely on your defensive abilities! The receiver's drops are met with tight net returns or net kills; smashes with tight net block returns or high lifts; clears with smashes or quick drops.

RECEIVING SERVES
(Fig 76)

Receiving positions are very similar to those adopted for serving – it is your intention to become the attackers immediately! The receiving 'base' is well forward with the non-racket foot just behind the front short service line. Do not compromise the attacking stance by standing further back anticipating flick and drive serves – you must be well forward to hit a low serve return as early as possible. The stance should be a 'position of immediate readiness', weight forward, racket in front of the head with the racket head at approximately top of net level. Be up on the toes, legs slightly bent on 'bouncy' knees, literally poised ready for launching. The partner equally takes up a position of readiness, just behind the receiver but still permitting a full view of both opponents and their court area. Above all, the stances of both receiver and partner should present a threatening image to the serving opponents.

Straight Low Serve Responses (Fig 77) If served loosely, that is two or three inches above the tape, hit down or flat with net kills, either straight or angled. If the delivery is very close to the tape play a very tight net return, either straight or angled. Maintain the front and back attacking formation. Only if these are not possible play a high lift, probably directed to one of the back corners, and very quickly move to the side-by-side defensive formation.

Angled low serve responses will require you to move probably more quickly but on the other hand will give you opportunities to hit wide of the opponents, employing the same shots as above and subsequent movement patterns.

Flick or drive serve responses The poised bouncy knee receiving attitude now allows you to explode up and backwards. Remember the one short, one long step basis of moving? Now make it one short bounce, one long leap! Despite the extreme pressure you must endeavour to respond with an attacking smash or very fast drop (slow will not do). Your partner will as quickly move in front of you to cover the court area now vacated and attack any loose returns to your shots. If taken unawares and unable to play a downwards shot then hit a high clear to one of the corners and move quickly with your partner into side-by-side defensive formation.

High serve responses There is only one way to deal with these – severely! Hard-hit smashes should produce either outright winners or easy pickings for your quickly moving forward partner. Very fast drops against the now side-by-side serving side will also produce dividends.

Up until this stage the rally has not advanced beyond the first two shots of serve and receive. Indeed at the initial lower levels of games play (as relative newcomers develop their technical and tactical skills) most rallies have been won, or lost, by this time. However with practice and greater experience, rallies become longer and partnerships have to develop attacking and defensive strategies.

ATTACKING SHOTS
The objectives of your doubles partnership will be to make your opponents cover the maximum area of their court in responding to your shots whilst minimising your movements. As mentioned earlier, one of the strongest elements must be the ability to serve in a variety of ways which allow your partnership to take on the attacking role immediately. Thereafter, you should endeavour to direct the majority of your shots quickly downwards playing all, if possible, but certainly the majority off the forehand.

Smashes should be in the majority, always directed steeply downwards and mainly away from the opponents; or from time to time aimed directly at them (possibly with a flatter trajectory). The primary objective is to beat them completely; the secondary to restrict the variety and quality of responses. Because you have two opponents your drops should also be played quickly, that is off the smash, rather than clear, action. Flat, sharply struck drives will also be employed, these to be played straight and wide of the opponents. With shots at the net the intention should always be to strike the shuttle down with net kills, wide of the opponents or, as with the smash, directly at their bodies; should this not be possible then tight net shots should be used. Clears, played with great discretion, can be used provided always that they are flat and fast.

DEFENSIVE SHOTS
Your opponents will have set themselves exactly the same objectives as you have. Your defending abilities must, therefore, be such that you can first blunt your opponent's attacks and then turn these to your advantage. Smashes should be returned positively, that is with the intent of moving your opponents, thus gaining an early reversal of advantage. Flat drive

73

Fig 76   Thomas Lund and Jon Holst-Christensen of Denmark showing how to receive service. No question here about their preparedness to move quickly into action once the service is delivered.

returns passing close to the top of the net, usually away from the centre, will prevent your opponents from srtiking down at the net or playing the second smash. Block returns, again usually away from the centre of the net, passing gently over and close to the top of the net, can achieve the same effect. Strongly struck high lifts towards the back boundary line, sensibly directed, can force your opponents to play their smashes under more pressure than they would wish. This is particularly so when the cross-court lift is employed to isolate one of your opponents, forcing him to undertake the bulk of the attack. Returns must be dealt with on a 'total commitment' basis – the first intention must always be to strike the shuttle down at the net, as your partner is there to cover the rest of the court if necessary. If failing in this objective, play tight net returns straight or along the net but always so that they oblige the opponents to move in response. Should it prove impossible to play either of these shots, then lift strongly

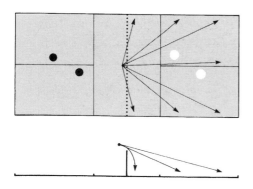

● Receiving team
○ Serving team

Fig 77 Returning serve – shot trajectories and placements.

and high towards the back boundary line so that your partnership can 'regroup' for the next attack. Your opponents may occasionally catch you unawares with a flat clear. In this situation, rather than being tempted into playing an off-balance (therefore poorly executed) smash or drop, the better strategy can be to play a positive high and deep clear in reply, thus gaining time to be better prepared for the next attack.

GENERAL COMMENT
The overall emphasis in the doubles games is on hitting the shuttle quickly. However, we should not forget our overall objective of making the opponents cover the maximum area of their court. Employing a 'one-paced' game eventually becomes too predictable and the 'predictable is exploitable'. Therefore, your partnership must learn to play with subtlety as well as speed, employing changes of both pace and direction when in both the attacking and defensive roles. Always endeavour to play the shuttle to those areas of the court which have just been vacated by your opponents, forcing them to play at speeds beyond their capabilities and/or disrupting their 'ideal' defending and/or attacking formations.

TRIANGULAR BASES
Here we will consider the possibility that two players can operate from a single base by observing fairly simple 'rules of conduct' which incorporate the two formations mentioned earlier, namely, attacking and defending. Obviously this base is a larger one than that used for singles and it has different shapes.
It has already been established that, in the serving and receiving situations, both

server and receiver will be in positions of readiness which are nearer to the net than those of their respective partners. One member of each pair has become the front player, the other the back player. Both pairs are in the attacking formation and positioned within 'bases' which are roughly right-angled triangles in shape. (Consider Fig 75; the back player has his feet across the bottom of the triangle the front player has his feet along the upright of the triangle – the receivers will have adopted much the same formation). The moment the serve is delivered each pair has to decide whether to maintain or break out of this formation. They cannot both stay in the attacking formation.

The *attacking formation* (Figs 78–9) of front and back is adopted immediately one member of your side moves to hit the shuttle down. All of the illustrations show an adherence to this roughly right-angled triangle shape. Both players have the same objective of hitting the shuttle steeply downwards, the back player to produce outright winners or loose, lifted responses for his forward partner. In turn the front player aims to finish off rallies with sharply hit down shots or other shots which will produce lifted shots for his partner's further attacks. Using the court centre line as the triangle's upright with the front player slightly to the left or right of this, the formation covers four contingencies. One, the front player allows his partner to see most, if not all, of the opponent's court; two, the front player is in a position to cut out hard driven defensive shots played away from his partner; three, the front player is in a good position to hit down any returns played back to the net; and four, the way is open for him to get back very quickly if needs be. Attacking formations are not fixed and static. Both

players are constantly moving, adjusting their positions in response both to shots played by the opponents and by their own positions. Their formation must be able to cover quickly not only the front and back areas of their court but also both sides.

To counter attacks from your opponents you will adopt the *defending formation* (Figs 79–81) to best manage responses to their attacking shots. Essentially, to defend you 'spread' yourselves across the base of the triangle, which you will recall is away from the front court area, to be side by side approximately mid-way between the net and the back boundary line. Both players now have the common objectives of defending their side of the court against attacks and converting this defence into attack at the earliest time. Again this formation is not static but is constantly mobile, adjusting in response both to shots played against it and the movements made by each player. All of the responses must be immediate and fast. Move quickly forward to take shots directed into the forecourt. Respond speedily with feet and racket, in that order, to the opponents' fiercest smashes into the mid-court. Move quickly backwards if fast flat attacking clears be employed against you.

CHANGING FORMATIONS

It will soon become obvious that within fast rallying situations there are very thin border-lines between the attacking and defending formations. The patterns of play are constantly and continuously changing. In the attacking formation, the back player should not be totally committed to the back, but be prepared to move quickly forward into the defending formation if this becomes necessary. Equally, the forward player should not be totally committed to

Fig 78   Thomas Lund and Jon Holst-Christensen again showing the advantages of preparing for explosive action. Jon counters a flick serve with a high leaping smash return. Thomas has quickly moved forward to become the front player to 'hunt' down any loose block returns.

Fig 79   Four English Internationals on court clearly illustrating the attack and defence formations. Chris Hunt jump smashes with Simon Archer moving quickly forward to counter any returns to the net from the Nick Ponting (on left) and Julian Robertson side-by-side defensive formation.

Fig 80   Four Indonesian players: Irianto and Kartona on attack – note the high jump smash – and Gunawan and Suprianto defending in the side-by-side formation.

Fig 81   Indonesian players again – this time Ricky Subagya (nearest camera) and Rexy Mainaky. It is obvious from their attention and racket preparation that a smash is being directed between their positions.

net play, but be prepared to move quickly back into the defending formation should the opponents' shots dictate this.

Conversely, when in the defending formation opportunities are constantly being presented for your side to adopt the attacking formation: for example, shots directed to your forecourt, flat clears towards your backcourt or when you are able to drive return smashes. All these open up possible opportunities to convert defence to attack. The opportunity to adopt the attacking formation must be taken immediately.

Accordingly, your formations, whether attacking or defending, must be fluid and flexible to ensure that neither member becomes isolated within the rally requiring the other to engage in a 'one against two' confrontation. It may be easier to overcome some of the complexities of court positional play by considering 'push-pull' and 'triangle defence' principles.

PUSH-PULL PRINCIPLES
(Fig 82)
Imagine that your partnership is linked by a rope that passes through a fixed point on your court. The 'rope' is infinitely variable between rigid and flexible and, as it is imaginary, you can pass through it. It is 'fixed' to a point which is on the centre line behind the front service line. When you are in the side-by-side defending formation the rope has an inverted 'V' shape and is taut.

If your partner moves straight backwards towards a high lifted shuttle, you will be pulled forward into the attacking formation. Your partner is allowed a full view of the opposite court. You are positioned to cut out hard-driven replies directed away from

79

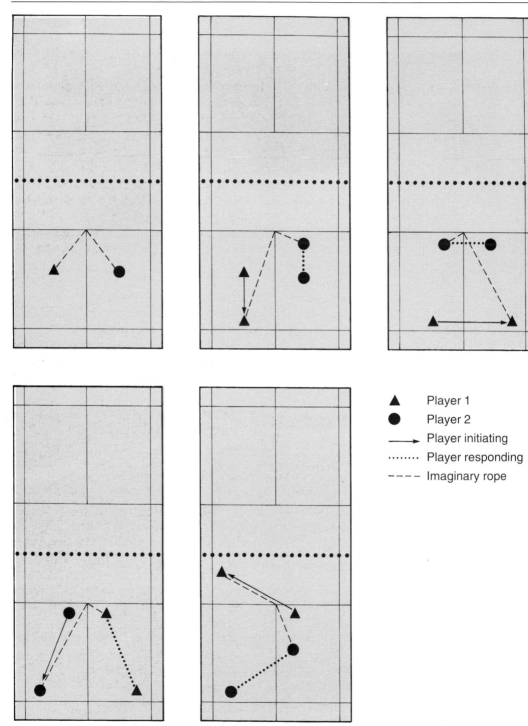

Fig 82   Level doubles – push-pull principles of court movement.

your partner, and to attack any shots directed into the forecourt.

Conversely if you initiate a change by moving forward to respond to a shot in your forecourt you will push your partner back into the attacking formation.

If the next shot from either of these situations is defensive, i.e. a clear rather than a smash or a lift, both of you will return to the original side-by-side defending formation by pushing and pulling one another into this position.

The imaginary 'rope' allows you to pass through thus avoiding situations where side-by-side formations are created for exploitation by your opponents. If you play a net shot on the right side of the net, then move quickly to a reply to the left side, your partner will be pulled to the side of the court that you have just vacated, and so on.

There are no specific rules, other than for serving and receiving, about which member of your partnership plays which shot next. Should your partner, when nearest the net, immediately move backwards to hit the next shot, then you can make way for him and allow yourself to be pulled forward to replace him as the forward attacking player. Do not consider the merits or otherwise of the move, just the principle of pushing and pulling. Some other examples of push-pull principles of movement are shown in the diagrams. The arrows indicate the initiating move, the dotted line the reaction.

TRIANGLE (WEDGE) DEFENCE
(Fig 83)
It was stated earlier that the defending formation called for the players to be side by side. Firstly, consider a situation in which the attacking player is preparing to hit a

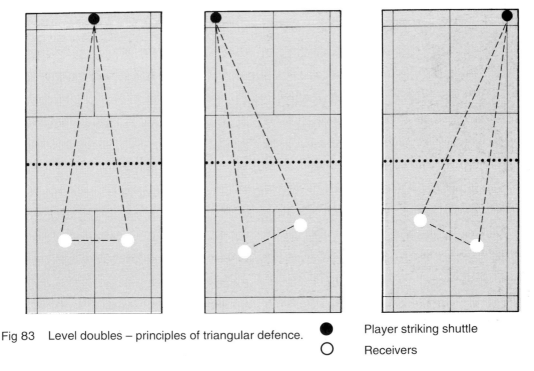

Fig 83   Level doubles – principles of triangular defence.

● Player striking shuttle
○ Receivers

81

smash or drop from immediately above the centre line. The defending players position themselves at the corners of the bottom line of a triangle, equidistant from the striker. If the shuttle is being hit from an extreme corner then the defenders should again adopt an equidistant triangle (or wedge) defence formation. This has the effect of placing each player approximately the same distance from the striker so they are better able as a pair to deal with both the straight and cross-court shots.

Mixed Doubles

Mixed doubles is the game most frequently played by club players. Almost invariably the partnership adopt a constant attacking formation once rallying, with the lady covering only shots to the forecourt and her partner covering the remainder of the court area. This is based on the assumption that men are usually stronger than ladies – though this is not always the case of course! Assuming that your partnership has agreed to this arrangement, we will, where necessary, consider separately the role of each partnership member. Otherwise, virtually all of the considerations applicable to level doubles attacking situations apply.

SERVING
(Figs 84 & 85)
Low serves from both players should be in the majority and mostly directed towards the T-junction of the front service line. Usually, returns of the serve to your forecourt will be dealt with by the lady; those lifted or pushed (driven) to the other areas of the court by the man. As early as possible during each game, each member should determine the responses of the opponents

to variations of the low serve, as very seldom will games be won by low serving alone. While these variations will not produce outright winners, they should have the effect of unsettling the receivers' responses, leading to loose returns. More importantly, they should consider their ability to reverse the opposing side's attacking formation by directing a large number of flick and drive serves to the opposing lady.

The lady will serve from the normal doubles serving position, that is, close to the front and centre lines, with her partner adopting a position of readiness which is close to her, but still permits a full view of the opponents and their court area. The man will usually serve from close to the centre line, but from further back so that the lady is in front of him, immediately able to deal with any of the opponents' subsequent returns to the forecourt. The lady usually takes up a position on the non-racket side of her partner as shown in the accompanying diagrams.

RECEIVING SERVES
Read again the section under Level Doubles on this subject, then implement the essential differences as outlined below.The lady deals with the opponents' low serves as she would in ladies' doubles but, thereafter, devotes her attentions to dealing only with replies directed to her forecourt. As in level doubles, flick and drive serves should be dealt with decisively but, above all, with regard to making the quickest possible recovery to her 'fixed' role as the front player. Smashes and drops should be played straight with good shot-making technique, enabling rapid forward recovery to deal with any returns to the forecourt. She will totally ignore any other shots such as a straight lift designed to keep her at the back of the

Fig 84   Chris Hunt and Gillian Clarke, English Internationals. Gillian is positioned to the left of the T-junction allowing Chris to see all of the receiver's court when serving from the right-hand court. Note Gillian's total concentration and position of immediate readiness.

Fig 85   Now note that although Chris is now serving from the left court Gillian has remained in much the same place. In both illustrations observe the great precision with which Chris is serving.

court! If unable to play either the smash or drop, a positive high clear across the court should be played to allow maximum time for recovery into a wedge defence formation. Particularly note that these shots are designed to allow the lady to move straight forward, i.e., take the shortest route back to the forecourt. Cross-court smashes and drops and straight clears are not excluded but should be played with discretion and a great certainty of how your partnership will cope with the ensuing possible responses.

The man should positively attack the op-ponents' low serves as often as possible without unduly compromising the partner-ship. To facilitate this, he will be well for-ward with his partner behind and to one side but close to him. When taking the low serve, it must always be his intention to hit the shuttle down, then immediately with-draw to his usual position in the court, leav-ing his partner moving quickly forward to deal with any returns to the net. Should he be obliged, by the quality of the low serve, to play a net return, this must be played with the intention of offering his partner the best opportunity both to move forward and then to play an attacking net shot. Flick and drive serves must be dealt with severely and directed with regard to drawing poor responses for himself or, again, his partner, who will be moving forward quickly. If all else fails, the positive clear should be played, allowing maximum time for him and partner to prepare themselves for the inevitable attack from their opponents. Above all, he must not play shots which enable the opponents to keep him at the front of the court thus compromising the partnership's mixed formation.

ATTACKING AND DEFENSIVE SHOTS

A great number of these are as outlined under Level Doubles. There are, however, notable differences between the two games as each requires more emphasis on some shots than others. In addition each member of the partnership will need to develop their individual abilities to play their particular shots in different ways. The game is played with both pairs constantly in attacking formations. Therefore, the centre of the court is well defended against cross-court shots and the sides of the court are most often exposed and open to attack. Shots towards the sides of the court will, therefore, be played frequently so both players in the partnership have to develop the ability to attack and defend on both sides of the body. For the man this means developing smashes and drops, flat attacking drives, drive returns to smashes and block returns to the net, all taken wide of both sides of the body, i.e. employing both forehand and, particularly, backhand shots. In addition to requiring a full repertoire of shots, he will also need to be fleet of foot, being obliged to cover the larger part of the partnership's court area. The lady must

develop an ability to attack any loose returns to the net, hitting these down whenever possible, playing tight net returns and quickly intercepting the opponents' drives.

GENERAL COMMENT

As in the level doubles game, the emphasis is upon hitting the shuttle quickly but, once again, subtlety, employed sensibly, will reap dividends. Endeavour always to incorporate changes of pace as well as direction into your game to upset the rhythm of your opponents' responses. It is difficult, if not impossible, for the lady to play net kills if her partner does not play shots which draw responses to the net. By the same token, if the lady constantly lifts the shuttle from the net, there will be few opportunities for her partner to hit the shuttle down.

BASING

(Figs 86 & 87)

The triangle basing, push-pull and wedge defence principles outlined for level doubles can be sensibly modified for use in mixed doubles. The essential consideration is that the lady must spend most of her time in front of her partner. Triangle basing will be in constant use as the lady, as the forward initiating player, constantly adjusts her position from one side or the other of the centre line. Push-pull principles apply when, for example, the lady is obliged to move towards the back of the court to receive flick, drive and high serves. Her movement backwards has the effect of 'pulling' her partner forward, if only momentarily, to cover the vulnerable cross-court front area. He will, of course, be immediately 'pushed' back when the lady, having played her return to the serve, moves quickly forward to regain her old

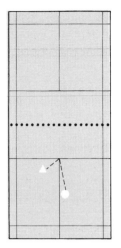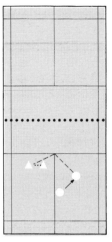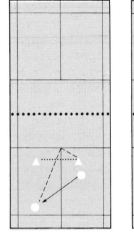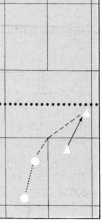

O Man
Δ Lady
⟶ Player initiating push-pull movement
..... Player responding
---- Imaginary rope

Fig 86 Mixed doubles – push-pull principles of court movement.

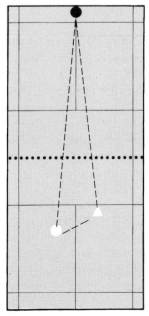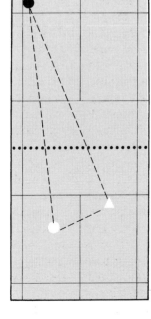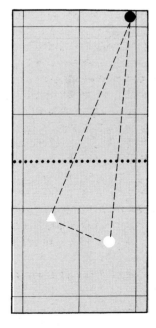

● Player striking shuttle
○ Man
△ Lady

Fig 87 Mixed doubles – principles of triangular defence.

85

position. In the same manner the man, having received a low serve and then moved back-wards, will 'pull' the lady back to her forward position. Triangle defence principles will be adopted whenever the partnership is obliged to lift the shuttle. Again, it must be remembered that the lady will want to be nearer to the net than her partner at all times. Accordingly, after her side lifts the shuttle to a corner of the opponent's court the lady quickly positions herself diagonally opposite to cut out downwards-hit cross-court shots. She may position herself further back in the court but, nonetheless, will be forward of her partner who will have positioned himself on the other side of the court to deal with any of the straight shots. The lady's intention is to cut out only the attacking shots and she must, therefore, strongly resist the temptation to move further backwards, thus compromising the mixed formation. In all situations, by employing combinations of all three principles, the members of the partnership should most often be on opposite sides of the centre line.

SUMMARY

Only basic tactics ('rules of conduct') have been outlined for doubles games. You will see them employed at the very highest levels of competitive play but soon realise that other elements are being introduced. The best players, through experience and discussion have devised 'specific rules' around and within the basics (*see* Chapter 6).

5
Advanced Stroke and Shot Making

Earlier instruction was devoted to 'basic' stroke and shot making. It is essential that these principles are practised assiduously to build a basic framework from which shot variations can be produced to frustrate and confuse your opponents further. In the section on Low Serving it was suggested that 'slice' could be used both to control the trajectory and change the the direction of the flight of the shuttle. These same principles can be used with most of the other shots. Players of other racket and/or ball games will be familiar with the principles of imparting top and bottom spin to a ball. You can achieve similar results with most types of shuttle, particularly the best feathers, by spinning it during its flight and so influencing its pace, direction and trajectory. You can greatly increase your repertoire of shots by adding slice to the standard range. We will consider its application for each of the basic shots.

Reminder – all of the descriptions of the shots are for the right-handed player. If you are left-handed then substitute left for right and vice versa.

Overhead Forehand Slice
(Figs 88 & 89)

Generally, the effect of slicing, in the direction dictated by the racket head throwing

and follow-after actions, accelerates the pace of the shuttle initially, produces a flatter trajectory and causes it to veer to the left. It is most effectively employed only with the downwards-hit shots. Remembering the need to disguise your intentions there must be no discernible changes in initial stroke and shot-making actions. The slicing effect is produced by hitting with the racket face 'closed' as opposed to the 'open face' applied to basic shots. In other words the outer edge of the head frame is nearer to the net than for the basic shots. It can be likened to endeavouring to hit the shuttle with the outer edge of the racket. Hand turning, uncocking and follow-after is strongly in the direction of, then across, the intended flight of the shuttle. The accompanying illustrations demonstrate this principle. Overhead forehand slice can be very effectively used to produce fast, swerving drops and smashes. These will be tighter to the net tape, have more vertical fall and land further in front of the opponent than anticipated. Also they will have gone across the front of, rather than directly at, the opponent, forcing him to change direction and arrive even later to play a counter.

Reverse slice, or cutting, to make the shuttle veer from left to right, can also be employed and is considered under Round the Head Shots.

Fig 88   Racket attitude for overhead forehand slice.

Fig 90   Racket attitude for overhead backhand slice.

Overhead Backhand Slice
(Figs 90 & 91)

The effect of slicing (racket head 'closed' with outer edge leading) when hitting overhead backhand shots is to make the shuttle veer from left to right. That, is the shuttle will travel faster initially, have a flatter trajectory and fall closer to the net. As, assuming correct stroke and shot making, there will be no follow-after of body and arm, slicing is produced solely by use of forearm and hand. The racket strings are 'drawn' diagonally across the base of the shuttle, from close to and away from the head. The accompanying illustrations demonstrate the principle. As with the forehand, the results will be fast, swerving drops and smashes across the opponent's front.

Underarm Slices

The results achieved by slicing either the forehand or backhand underarm shots are similar and there are three ways in which we can use slicing actions to advantage.

UNDER-CUTTING
(Fig 92)

This is used when replying to the opponent's steeply downward smashes to reduce the speed of the returns dramatically and send them steeply down after pasing over the net. The racket face is presented at an angle which puts the bottom edge closest to the net and is then moved downwards to meet the shuttle in an 'under-cutting' movement. This produces a block return but with a slow looped trajectory as shown in Fig 92. It can be coupled with turns of the racket face to left or right to create angled sliced blocks.

TOP SLICING
(Fig 93)
This is a method of responding to an opponent's flatter smashes directed to either side of your body with equally fast and flat, straight or angled returns. It is difficult to employ top slice effectively against steeply angled smashes. The intention is to top-spin drive the returns to make them 'loop' downwards after passing flat over the net. Employing basic backhand and forehand driving actions, the racket head is slightly angled, top edge nearest to net and below intended point of impact. As the shuttle is hit, at the end of powerful arm swinging, the racket head follows after in a forwards and upwards direction. The actions should be underarm but overhand and similar to shots used in the games of tennis and table-tennis. The accompanying diagram illustrates the principles and desired effects.

UPWARDS SLICING
(Figs 94–6)
Upwards slicing achieves a similar result to top slicing but is used to return smashes aimed directly at your body. It can only be played with what approximates to a backhand action and grip. Stand in the basic position of readiness, body and feet square to the smasher with elbow up to bring the racket hand in front of the body at about chest height. The racket head is straight down, held in a backhand grip so that racket face is 'open' to the smash. The hitting action is produced by drawing the racket very quickly up and slightly forward while keeping the head vertically downwards, like drawing a long sword out of a scab-

bard! Make this movement so fast that your feet are lifted off the floor. Drawing the strings up and across the base of shuttle will impart spin, the faster the movement the greater the spinning effect. This movement and the spinning effect achieved produce flat, hard drive returns which dip as they pass over the net.

Round the Head Shots
(Figs 97–100)

As the title suggests, these are shots which are above head height but wide of the left-hand side of the body. They oblige you to take the racket face round and behind, or sometimes across the face of, the head in order to hit the shuttle. Particular examples are receiving low drive serves down the backhand side of the body or playing overhead forehand shots out of the backhand rear court area when under pressure. In the first instance you are obliged to play the shot as it is forced upon you. But when shots are directed high to the backhand rear court you have a choice, either to play overhead backhand or round the head shots. If just sufficient time is available round the head forehand shots may be a stronger option than your range of overhead backhand shots. They also have an advantage over backhands in allowing you to continue to look towards the opponents.

As we are considering a slightly different technique it is necessary to refer back to earlier descriptions of overhead forehand shots. These defined a striking attitude where both right foot and shoulder are behind the shuttle immediately prior to moment of impact. Attempting to play round the head shots with this technique will prove difficult, if not impossible, as the head will be in the way of the arm. It will also be

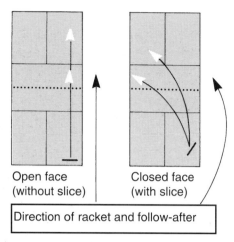

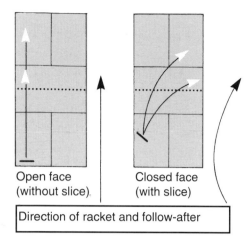

Fig 89   Principles of overhead forehand slice.

Fig 91   Principles of overhead backhand slice.

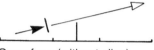

Open face (without slice)

Open face (without slice)

Partially closed face with under slicing

Partially closed face with top slicing

Fig 92   Under-cutting.

Fig 93   Top slicing.

Open face (without slice)

Partially closed face with upwards slicing

Fig 94   Upwards slicing.

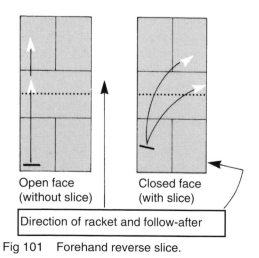

Fig 101   Forehand reverse slice.

Fig 95   Upwards slicing – preparation. Note angle of arm allowing racket head to be taken down below waist level.

Fig 96   Upwards slicing – hitting. The strength of the upwards movement has lifted the feet off the floor.

very difficult to achieve a balanced forward recovery. Both of these problems can be overcome if we change only one element of the striking attitude, which is to hit the shuttle off the left (non-racket) foot. Preceding elements, of adapting the overhead forehand striking attitude, moving back with racket foot leading, remain unchanged. At the moment of striking, the non-racket foot is placed beneath and well behind the intended point of impact, upper body movement is employed to bring the left shoulder back, and the arm and racket throwing elements are now no longer impeded. You should now be able to play any of the forehand overhead shots to any point of the opponent's court area. It must be realised

that in overcoming one problem, we have created another. The left foot is now further back in the court than would be the case with the basic overhead forehand action. Recovery forward is accelerated by vigorously throwing the right leg and foot out in front of and towards base.

Reverse Slice
(Fig 101)

As its name suggests, this calls for the slicing action to be in the reverse direction to the overhead forehand slice described earlier. The effect is to make the shuttle swerve from left to right. Usually, therefore, it is used from the left (backhand) side of

91

Fig 97   Round the head forehand – usual forehand attitude.

Fig 98   Upper body turning. The left (non-racket) foot is being placed behind the body and the left shoulder is brought back to allow the racket arm to pass across the face.

Fig 99   Hitting. The racket arm has now passed in front of the face with the shuttle being taken over and in front of the left shoulder.

Fig 100   Recovery. With the left foot firmly on the floor the right leg is 'kicked' forward to accelerate forward recovery.

the court, and with a round the head action. Immediately prior to hitting the shuttle, the racket face is closed by using the hand to turn the racket edge nearest the head towards the net, whilst at the same time moving the entire outstretched arm across the face. As this action slows the flight of the shuttle, the arm action must be fast to induce more pace into the shot.

Shots at the Net

There are a number of other shots, in addition to those already described, that can be employed at the net. Before looking at these we should consider a further basic technique, namely the net play striking attitude. This is rarely, if ever, employed in the singles game but is an essential requirement in the doubles games for the player in the forward attacking position.

NET PLAY STRIKING ATTITUDE
(Figs 102–105)
Adopt the position of readiness described earlier, weight carried easily on feet approximately shoulder width apart behind the short service line. The distance back is determined by a number of factors, specifically height and experience but, it is suggested, you should observe an unwritten rule which dictates that you never place the non-racket foot in front of the short service line. Instead you reach out with a long lunge from the position of readiness. As the net is five feet high and your intention is always to hit the shuttle down, the racket face should be kept at about that level at all times. The racket is held with neither forehand or backhand grips, but between both in what is known as the 'pan-handle' grip. This will ensure that an 'open face' is always presented to oncoming shuttles. Far too many

players use the wrist forcefully when hitting the shuttle close to the net, leading to the possibility of striking the net, (a fault) but also to a high percentage of shuttles being hit into the net. Therefore most of these net shots should be produced with quick pushing forwards movements of hand and arm ensuring that the racket face stays almost vertical throughout. When shuttles are high enough to hit down your shots are produced with quick 'tapping' movements of the racket end – you hit with the tips of the fingers! The accompanying photographs clearly show the requirements for the net play striking attitude. From this position, shots can be hit down to the right side, in front of and to the left side of the body, spanning a considerable area of the net. Movement to shots wider than this should be made by quickly side-stepping to left or right without changing the attitude. Using this technique you should, with practice, be able to strike the shuttle sharply down straight or with small changes of the racket head angle, to the left or right. Tight net shots can be produced by employing a 'dead racket', i.e. little or no movement of the racket – allowing the shuttle to bounce gently off and over. As the racket arm is pushed forward to play these shots, pulling the arm quickly back ensures that the racket head is always up, prepared immediately for the next shot. A further bonus is that the shuttle can be seen right onto the racket by having this up in front of the face. By side-stepping along the net you will not be reduced to 'running the net' (first playing a wide forehand then being made to run across to play a wide backhand, and so on). Instead, you will be constantly on balance, racket up, prepared always to hit shuttles down, and above all, in command!

Of course, your opponents will not

Fig 102　Shots at the net – preparation. Note 'totally square to the net' attitude and pan-handle grip.

Fig 103　Hitting to the front. The racket arm has been straightened quickly without employing wrist action.

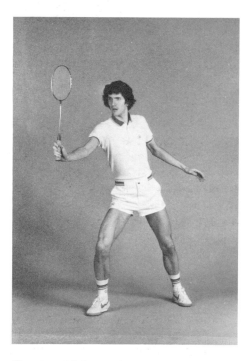

Fig 104　Hitting to the right. With only a small movement of the feet the racket arm has been extended to the right in exactly the same manner as in Fig 103.

Fig 105　Hitting to the left. Again a small movement of the feet with the racket arm extended across the front of the body.

always allow you opportunities to hit the shuttle down in the ways described above. In this case there are three other shots, the stab, tumble and brush net shots, which may also be used. Basic lunging movements for these were described under Net Returns in Chapter 3. They may be played off either forehand or backhand.

THE STAB
(Fig 106)
To produce the stab net shot the arm is straightened quickly with the racket head slightly lower than the hand at point of impact and a final 'stabbing' motion produced so that a degree of slice is imparted to the shuttle. The effect is for the shuttle to 'pop-up' sharply on your side of the net but to fall steeply and tightly down the net on the opponent's side.

THE TUMBLE
Initial preparation for the tumble is precisely the same as for the stab, but the slicing action is from one side to the other with the racket face parallel to the floor. This allows you to play the shot very close to the net but without touching it. When played correctly, the effect is to make the shuttle turn over, base above feathers or skirt, staying close to the tape and then to tumble down the other side of the net. Essentially the shuttle is out of control for a short part of its travel. This shot is very difficult to counter as your opponent has to allow the shuttle to fall below the bottom of the net before being able to attempt a return.

THE BRUSH
The brush net shot is played with the racket face above the hand in an upright attitude – see Fig 102. The hitting action is from left to right, or vice versa, using a fast brushing, or

Fig 106 Attitude for stab net shot. An extended lunge with almost straight arm – note angle of the racket head.

wiping, action of the hand. As always, when the racket strings are drawn across the base the shuttle is made to spin. This causes the shuttle to travel into the opponent's court with an initial flat trajectory, which quickly becomes steeply downwards depending upon the amount of slice applied.

Double Motion
(Figs 107 & 109)

One further variation which can be introduced and applied to most, if not all shots (serves excluded because of the Laws) is that of employing 'double motion' prior to striking. Here the intention is that by intro-

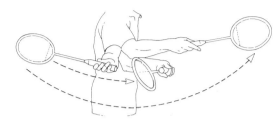

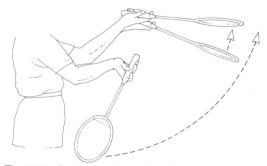

Fig 107   Double motion; the apparent high lift has become a tight net return.

Fig 108   Double motion; after threatening to play a hard, straight drive, a cross-court return to the net is played.

ducing a preliminary movement of the racket prior to hitting the shuttle, the opponent is led to believe that one shot will be played only to find that another results. Two examples follow.

1. (Fig 107) You move very quickly towards an opponent's drop to the net and produce a powerful movement suggestive of a high lift, stop the racket short of the impact point then start again to produce a tight net return. Or try the reverse of this. 'Show' a soft net shot then quickly flick the racket head back and up to produce a high lift.
2. (Fig 108) You suggest, with an apparently powerful action, that you are about to play a hard, straight drive then stop the racket short of impact and start again, this time to play a soft block return to the net. The reverse of this is to 'show' a soft block return then with a quick flick of hand and racket head send the shuttle quickly up towards the rear of the court.

This principle can be applied to most shots. Some of the very best players extend the concept further by using triple motion with some of their shots. Once their opponents have learned to anticipate the results of their double motion shots they revert to the 'original' shot.

Note You are again reminded that double and triple motion hitting cannot be employed with any of the serves.

6
Advanced Games Play

Chapter 4 introduced basic tactics – rules of conduct – for the three different forms of games play. Certain statements bear repeating; they are:-

1. Tactics are logical solutions to situations actually encountered in games play.
2. In addition to allowing you to exploit your opponents' deficiencies, tactics must also protect your inadequacies.
3. Whilst the principles of basic tactics are valid at all levels of play (including the very highest) they must be subject to adaption to suit individuals and circumstances.

All too often players assume a better understanding of tactics to be a panacea allowing them to overcome deficiencies in stroke and shot making, court movement and general fitness. In actual games play they soon learn otherwise, as more experienced and capable opponents will quickly expose any such deficiencies. Even basic tactics, therefore, assume that the players have most, if not all, of the essential attributes required by the complete badminton player. Certainly, a better appreciation of tactics will help you to win more often than lose. However, practising and perfecting shots, court movements and general fitness should not be neglected, otherwise you will be unable to apply this better appreciation successfully. Basic tactics offer simple sets of 'rules of conduct' for the player in the singles game, or pairs of

players in doubles games. To these basic rules players must add further individually specific supplementary ones. These extra rules serve two purposes. They enable you and/or your side to utilise strengths while protecting your weaknesses. Equally they should allow you to attack the opponents' weaknesses and avoid playing to their strengths. Even then the rules have some degree of flexibility which will allow amendment during actual competitive play. The following comments are, therefore, logical suggestions rather than dogmatic rules. In practice you will find that they can well serve you just as they are written or that you may wish to make slight modifications to suit your specific requirements.

PREPARING TO PLAY

You should ensure that prior to playing, whether this be a practice, club or match game, body temperature and pulse rate have been raised and that you have practised those shots which will be most applicable to the particular game about to be played. There are two separate elements to consider, warming-up and knocking-up.

Warming-up

Prior to playing, perform a programme of exercises to generally warm the body, increase the pulse rate and stretch muscles. Chapter 8 offers suggestions on this subject. Under no circumstances should you make a cold start. Quite apart from the possibility of sprains and strained muscles resulting from violent movement being imposed on cold ligaments and muscles, it is essential that the cardio-respiratory (heart and lung) rate is raised to that approximating to the requirements of the forthcoming event.

Knocking-up

Very little time is allowed for this before playing a game, particularly at tournaments when, usually, only three minutes are allowed. Consequently it is essential that you have well considered and rehearsed knocking-up programmes related specifically to the game to be played. While all of the programmes will have common elements, more emphasis will be placed on some of the shots than others. In the singles game you must, sometimes unfortunately, rely on your opponent to assist with your knocking-up. However, he will have the same objectives as you and, most probably, a very similar schedule of shots to practise. Start with some high clears to loosen the upper body and to establish the amount of effort required to 'clear the length' of the court depending on the hall's environment, speed of shuttle and so on. Practise both forehand and backhand shots, ensuring you incorporate full travel-to and recovery footwork. Then introduce some drops followed by smashes. Your opponent will want to practise them also allowing you an opportunity to try your returns to these shots. Finally practise both high and low singles serves. Throughout the knock-up you should also be endeavouring to gauge your opponent's responses to your shots. Any final decisions may have to be 'qualified' as your opponent may not have revealed his entire hand or may have flattered to deceive.

Knocking up for the doubles games should always be conducted against your partner, never with an opponent. As with your tactics, preliminary discussions and rehearsals will ensure that you have a programme which fully covers all your shot requirements. You could sensibly incorporate some practice routines. Again start with clears to loosen the upper body but not too many. Then engage in a short rally incorporating drops, net returns and lifts, followed by a similar rally to introduce smashes. Practise net shots and retrieving these in a game-like situation to quicken the responses of both front and mid-court player. Finally both players should practise low serves and receiving them.

SERVING

General

Determine as early as possible the responses of your opponent to all your serves. If well versed in the singles game, for example, your opponent will have developed strong, positive responses to high serves; in doubles games most receivers will anticipate that you will serve low and to the centre. How does the opponent respond to something different? Having tried and established which form of serve is most productive – you usually win the ensuing rally – continue with this but with discretion. Do not allow the opponent to become too accustomed to one form of serving but use variations to break up the rhythm of receiving. In the doubles game remember to serve for your partner as well as yourself. Your serves should provide early attacking opportunities for your side. The moment a serve fails to do so and your side comes under pressure then employ other serves. Above all, remember that the rules allow you reasonable time to prepare for, and that you can only score when, serving. Not taking time to serve and delivering shuttles into the net, out of court or straight onto the racket of the receiver will ultimately cost you the game.

The server must therefore be capable of serving in a variety of manners which:

1. Make the receiver move his racket or body but preferably both in order to return serve.
2. Force the receiver to move more quickly than he wishes and/or in directions which he finds difficult to recover from quickly.
3. By experimentation determine how best to draw poor responses from the receiver.
4. Pay regard to the capabilities of both himself and, in the doubles games, his partner.

In all cases the server (serving pair) must be immediately ready to maintain any advantage gained from the serve. Serving stance(s), dictated by the Laws, should be maintained only until the shuttle has been delivered. Thereafter, server (and partner when appropriate) should immediately leap into action, remembering the preparatory bounce into, or onto, 'base'.

RECEIVING

General

Only very rarely will servers deliver 'aces', rather, they will always assume that the serve will be returned. Their serves will therefore attempt to dictate the manner in which you, the receiver, respond with a view to attacking your returns at the earliest moment.

There are a number of ways in which the receivers can prevent this. One way is to adopt a stance of immediate readiness, weight biased slightly forward to allow quick leaps forward, with racket above hand, to attack the low service. Or, as quickly, to move back to counter high serves, flicks and drives, or sideways to angled and drive serves. Cultivate the habit of 'digging the toes' into the floor on slightly bent knees dynamically poised to explode into action. Hold the racket in a loose 'pan-handle' grip so that all of the face is presented to the server. The receiving position is determined by the form of games played. For doubles play it should be as far forward as possible; the best players, very deliberately, place the non-racket foot almost onto the front line and adopt the most intimidating of stances. The primary objective is to hit shuttles down whether hard or softly. In singles play the receiving position is further back but not so far that low serves cannot be quickly reached.

The receiver must be capable of dealing with the serves in ways which have, literally, the same objectives as the server, namely:

1. To move the server away from his base, while allowing a quick recovery to his own.
2. To make the server move more quickly than desired and/or in directions which inconvenience him.
3. By experimentation, find ways to draw poor responses to his returns.
4. Pay regard to the capabilities of both himself and, in the doubles game, his partner.

99

Singles

As the opponent has to cover the entire singles court area, serve returns should, most often, be directed to points furthest away from the server, most obviously the extreme corners.

When a low serve is received this is achieved by playing tight net returns to the forecourt corners or high lifts to extreme rear-court corners. If able to take the serve very early, aim directly at the server, if not to beat him completely, at least to restrict his replies. Be wary of hitting the early-taken serve too wide of the server, as this brings the shuttle within the span of a freely swinging racket, and a return which may be faster than you wish.

When the high serve is received, use drops to the extreme forecourt corners, clears to the extreme rear-court corners and smashes wide of the now centrally based opponent. Again you may find that a particular opponent deals less well with shots directed down the centre of the court whether these be to the fore-, mid- or back-court areas.

Do not overlook the effects of different paces and trajectories: for example, slow and looped drops compared with fast and flatter drops; high clears which take longer to reach the back court than those with fast, flat trajectories or smashes with steep or flat trajectories, with or without slice.

Doubles

The objective must be to attack the serve at all times – lifting shuttles being totally alien to your side's plan of conduct. Both receiver and partner will be in the receiving attitude of immediate readiness, instantly prepared to move once the serve is struck. The receiver will be well forward with the non-racket foot close to the front service line. (There must be no question of compromise in this situation, particularly from the lady in mixed doubles – otherwise you have immediately forsaken the first opportunity to attack.) When receiving serve aim to achieve at least one of the following. Either hit the shuttle sharply down with a view to scoring an outright winner or play a downwards or flat return forcing your opponents both to move and make a lifted response; that is, draw a reply which ensures that your side is immediately able to adopt its attacking formation. Only at very low levels of competition will a lifted response into the very back of the court gain any form of advantage. At higher levels playing a lift is tantamount to giving away the rally!

In both forms of doubles, the serving side will usually have adopted an attacking formation, thus leaving areas to their front and sides into which the receiver can quickly place the shuttle. Loose, low serves passing well above the net tape must be taken very early at the top of the net, and dealt with severely. Either hit them hard and aim at the bodies of either of the serving pair or hit down to left or right of their positions; or take them quickly and gently redirect away from the server with an angled net return. Very tight low serves should again be taken early, employing the brush net shot to hit down or flat into the opponent's court, or a stab or tumble net shot to draw a loose net return or lift from the incoming server.

Flick serves are dealt with by using open-faced or sliced smashes or drops directed down the sides of the court or, from time to time and with discretion, down the centre between the defending opponents. These responses will not always be outright winners but should draw loose returns for your

Fig 109   Susi Susanto of Indonesia, undoubtedly one of the world's greatest ladies singles players, at full stretch replying to a drop into her forecourt.

forward partner to 'hunt down' in the forecourt.

Respond to drive serves with a round the head flat smash or drop in the same manner as the flick. Again the receiver's partner will have moved forward to deal with any returns directed into the forecourt.

Occasionally your opponents may employ the singles action high serve. Your replies to these should be such (for example powerful smashes) that they soon learn not to use that particular serve in future.

RALLYING

Too often players assume that tactics serve only to identify places in which they should stand on court during rallies or, in doubles games, will establish whose turn it is to strike the shuttle next. From the outset, it is essential to realise that, other than when serving or receiving, no player becomes motionless on court but is constantly on the move. This may involve no more than bouncing on the toes but at no time should players allow themselves to come to a complete standstill – constant mobility is the key to instant responses!

Equally, in the doubles game, whilst it should be obvious within a rally which of the players is to hit the shuttle next, both players must be equally prepared to move to it. In all forms of doubles play, and particularly when defending, there will be some degree of 'shadowing' (covering one another) by each member of the partnership. As greater understanding develops, as a consequence of regularly playing with one another, the need for shadowing will be reduced and, ultimately, with total understanding, eliminated.

The following observations, on each of the three forms of game, are intended to be logical recommendations rather than absolute dogmas, and aim to promote thoughtful consideration of some aspects of each game. They should be considered only as guidelines as ultimately each player, or pair of players, must develop their quite specific rules. In considering these it will be realised that they very often illustrate not only how you can successfully conduct your game but, conversely, how not to! You will also have to develop the ability not only to observe your opponents' court movements, shot making techniques and changes in tactics during play, but also to respond in-stantly to these.

Singles

Firstly, it is important that the principles of

'bias basing' are fully understood and introduced into your singles game. These, when coupled with considerations of serving and receiving, will allow you to successfully play the singles game to quite a high level. However, they form only the basic framework from which you have to develop your own, very specific, rules of conduct. Even then, these specific rules may have to be adapted for individual opponents and circumstances. Bear in mind that there has to be an assumption that you are extremely fit and have a complete repertoire of shots. Should you be lacking in fitness, you must enter into a specific programme of training as, given

that your opponent is equally skilled, his superior fitness will prevail. Given two equally fit players, usually the more skilled of these will win.

ATTACKING THE BACKHAND

Most players are less strong and varied from the extreme backhand corner of the rear court. Determine which shots the opponent plays off his overhead backhand particularly when obliged to play these under pressure from your fast movements and shots. Are opportunities available for you to attack drops to your forecourt or 'short of a court length' clears to your rear court? Are the opponent's otherwise good

Fig 110 Arbi of Indonesia, one of the world's top singles players, moving quickly forward to play a backhand lift from the forecourt.

Fig 111 Rashid Sidek of Malaysia showing his leaping powers as he prepares to play a round the head forehand smash.

shots gained at the expense of late recovery allowing quickly played cross-court shots to gain you an advantage? Does he favour round the head forehands from the backhand corner, with good results but, again, late recovery allowing early exploitation? Learn to attack the backhand corner but also ensure that you can adequately resist similar pressure.

ANTICIPATION

To anticipate means to regard as likely, expect, forsee. Most players have favoured and usually quite instinctive responses in certain situations. These are usually one of their strongest shots, for example the heavy straight smash down your backhand following a high serve or a fast, sliced cross-court drop following a straight backhand clear. Once such favoured responses have been determined, do not be afraid of them, rather, on the basis of what is predictable is exploitable, make use of the knowledge gained. Serve high, anticipate the smash down your backhand, and respond with a cross-court block to the net well away from the opponent. After hitting a straight backhand clear, recover quickly to base, knowing that you can expect the cross-court drop, to play a straight net return.

Rarely do players hit the shuttle to the same place twice in succession. Using this knowledge with discretion allows you to reduce the amount of court that you will be required to cover next. For example, your opponent, having played his shot to your backhand will often respond to your reply with a shot directed elsewhere into your court area. He is achieving his aim of making you cover large areas of court. However, you can anticipate that he will not hit to your backhand with his next shot. This leaves only three corners to consider and

this may be reduced further by a knowledge of his favoured shots. As always, speed of recovery to base is essential but now with regard to covering areas of the court other than that just vacated!

BALANCING OR MANOEUVRING SHOTS

'Balancing' or 'manoeuvring' shots, while apparently negative, can produce rewards. These are those shots which are clearly not within the attacking category, but by the same token are not truly defensive. They serve to prolong a rally deliberately, either to tire the opponent and/or until a better opportunity is available for mounting an attack. Examples are constantly placing the shuttle to the back of the opponent's court with clears or with lifts from his drops, net returns and smashes.

PACE AND RHYTHM

Changing the pace and rhythm of play can yield worthwhile dividends. Here we are not only considering one or two shots within a rally, but conducting a number of rallies, possibly an entire game, at a different pace.

Often your opponents are fast response players, that is, they thrive on fast movement and shot making with the hope that this fast pace overwhelms you. This can be curbed by employing very high and deep clears and/or lifts from the net, by constantly serving high and playing slow, provided they are tight, drops. These shots increase the interval between the shuttle leaving your racket and arriving at your opponent's, thus breaking the fast response rhythm.

Conversely, you can upset the rhythm of the slower response player by employing fast, flat clears and shallow lifts from the net, a high proportion of low serves and variations and smashes and fast drops (both open-faced and sliced). These shots reduce the interval between hits and force the opponent to play at an unaccustomed pace.

ASSESSING THE OPPONENT

Each opponent can present differing problems requiring early solution if you are to impose your game, and will, upon them before they impose theirs upon you. A number of stratagems have already been suggested. However, realisation of the need to employ these may come too late in the game for you to make full use of them, perhaps even to introduce them! You can achieve early realisation of the best tactics to employ by segmenting the opponent's court, and defining the segments as positive and negative areas. The segmentation must be both horizontal and vertical, i.e., three-dimensional, not simply plan view. Initially, divide the court into four floor areas, front and back and forehand and backhand. After a number of rallies, you should be able to make a preliminary assessment regarding the area producing the best results for you, either outright winners or poor returns; conversely, you should have found the least productive area. Obviously, you then direct a large proportion of your shots, as often as possible, to the 'positive' area, while endeavouring to avoid playing to the 'negative' (least productive) area. As the game progresses you may have to 'fine tune' your original judgment with vertical segmentation of low, mid and high. For example, you determine that very positive results are achieved when you play shots to the rear backhand segment. As your opponent realises your intent, he counters these with increasing success. You then determine that shallow lifts and flat clears (mid vertical) played to that area bring more positive results than do high lifts and clears (high

vertical) thus redressing the situation. You may eventually feel the need to divide the opponent's court area into even smaller segments as the game progresses, or decide that certain areas can only sensibly be attacked following a particular sequence of shots. This concept can also be applied to doubles games but bear in mind that segmentation then is greater, with many more and smaller units, and that you must consider the pair in unison as well as individuals as you search for 'positive' and 'negative' areas.

Level Doubles

Earlier sections covered common elements of both level and mixed doubles and the obvious differences. This section offers other more specific suggestions for consideration – again they must not be seen as dogmas.

All of the considerations outlined for singles play are applicable to level doubles. In addition, thought must be given to your side having to deal with two players. For example, only one of your opponents may be less strong and varied from the backhand corner. Your side will have to manoeuvre that player into that position before using 'attacking the backhand' tactics. Each opponent may have different favoured, instinctive responses in certain situations which will have to be determined before applying ideas from the Anticipation section.

VERBAL AND VISUAL COMMUNICATION

These are essential ingredients of doubles play. Discussion of basically uncomplicated plans of intended action are essential if two players are to play 'as one'. Little time is available for this once on the court, so pairs regularly playing together must make time before and after matches to discuss their plans of operation, how effective or otherwise these were, modifications required, and so on. Each player must endeavour to, in the words of a once popular song, 'emphasise the positive' by establishing means of more often playing to the partnership's combined and individual strengths and preventing their weaknesses, again combined and individual, from being exposed. Once into a match situation time, albeit short, is also available between rallies and games for brief exchanges of ideas regarding tactics. More importantly, during games play each member of the partnership should verbally encourage and prompt the other. Verbal *encouragement* is the keyword as your partner will hardly need reminding of shot making errors or inaccuracies in placement. You are unlikely to beat two opponents alone once you have lost your partner's commitment to your side's endeavours! In rallies you can verbally prompt each other to reach the (seemingly) unreachable shuttle or define responsibilities with sharp, and timely, calls of 'yours' or 'mine'. Also assist with clear, positive called judgments regarding shuttles that may be falling out of court.

Also employ visual cues by always moving promptly to take up attacking or defensive positions. Obviously, one part of the court quickly filled by your partner is a clear indication that you must fill the other. The front player should initiate the changes of position resulting from either the attacking or defending formations, thus avoiding the danger associated with a player turning to look behind (see below).

COURT POSITIONS
The player nearest to the net dictates court positions when changing from the attacking to the defensive formations, and subsequent court formation changes. The player at the front of the court must always look forwards, firstly to reduce the response times to shots played to the net and, very importantly, because turning round to observe the partner's activities could result in being struck in the face by any mishit shot from the partner. Both players will be adjusting their positions at the dictate of shots being played and received by them in accordance with the basic tactics described earlier. In the event of either player playing a defensive shot, allowing their opponents to attack, the player at the front moves directly backwards, the partner moving to one side, if necessary, to permit this. Further, should the front player in playing an attacking shot decide immediately, (remember – no hesitation) that the return will be played straight back allowing that same player a further attacking shot, the partner will permit this by moving to one side and then forward to replace his partner at the front. The rule is a simple one – the front player, whether right or wrong at the time, dictates changes of formation. If there is disagreement it is a subject for later off-court discussion and possible revision of your partnership's book of rules.

FORWARD PLAYER
The forward player should never be astride the service line T-junction. Basing astride it when in the forward attacking position will both restrict your partner's sight of all the opponents' court, therefore the area into which he can play shots, and leave open for your opponents' returns a large area of your own court.

The forward player should always base behind the front service line and to the left

105

or right of the centre line as dictated by 'push-pull' principles. Basing too closely to the net will severely reduce response times, limit shot options, increase the distance to be travelled to move to the defensive formation and could also lead to a situation where the forward player is isolated from rallies. The actual forward base position is determined by considering both the above factors and relating these to the height of the player (the taller player can be further back and still be capable of stretching to reach net shots) and an individual's fast reaction and response ability (some players are naturally faster).

ONE PLAYER ATTACKING

Allowing only one player to maintain an attacking rally can pay dividends. Quite often shots from the back player can surprise his forward partner as much as the opponents, for example, the well-disguised drop. Furthermore, good technique incorporating rapid forward recovery places the back player as near, if not nearer, to the possible responses than his partner. In these circumstances it serves the partnership best to allow the back player to continue the attack without regard to existing formations. Consider the following. The shuttle has been lifted to the forehand area of the back court, one member of the partnership has arrived in good time to play any of a number of options, his partner has quickly taken up a forward position on the other side of the centre line. The striker plays a straight shot, either smash or drop, with good recovery and, having anticipated a straight return, continues forward to hit again. Providing the striker's move forwards is immediate, and his partner is not standing too far forward, he will visually signal his presence to his partner who will as immedi-ately move backwards to maintain the attacking formation.

SLEEPING PARTNER

Avoid becoming a 'sleeper' within rallying situations. Mention was made earlier of the need for both players to be constantly on the move and for the forward player not to become isolated. The possibility of becoming a 'sleeper' exists from the instant the first shot in a rally is hit. For example, your partner serves low, this is taken early by the opponent and hit quickly at your body. Having failed to prepare immediately the shuttle left your partner's racket you have been caught immobile and 'napping' and are unable to respond. Much the same possibility exists in long rallies despite, ostensibly, being continuously on the move. For whatever reason, you have been excluded from the rally for a number of shots when, suddenly, the shuttle is hit in your direction. Although only excluded for a short time you are out of touch with the pace of hitting and miss, or mishit, the shuttle. You have been caught out as the 'sleeper'. Mention was made earlier of 'shadowing' (a partner's shots) which can assist to overcome the 'sleeper' problem. Perhaps a better alternative is to employ some elements of the paragraph below.

'HUNTING THE SHUTTLE'

There is a constant danger of the forward attacking player's first becoming isolated and then a 'sleeper'. He should therefore adopt a policy of constantly looking for opportunities to hit the shuttle whether the shot is correctly his or not. He should 'hunt' for the chance, even half chance, to cut out the opponent's quickly hit passing shots whether straight or cross-court. These shots need not be hard struck. Usually it is enough to reach the shuttle with a dead racket to play a soft return to produce outright winners or to upset the rhythm of your opponents' play.

CROSS-COURT SHOTS

Whenever cross-court shots are used they must be played with great discretion and have regard to both positive and negative effects. From the fore- and mid-courts they can produce outright winners provided they are played away from one or both opponents. Hit down quickly from the mid- and rear courts they can again be used successfully when both opponents are biased more to one side or the other, or when the front player is ideally positioned to cover the usual straight block return. Cross-court drops, however, can often cause problems for your partner if the opponents reach them. Quite apart from the silently struck shot taking your partner by surprise, he must now cover the possibility of a straight net shot. This leaves your side exposed at two extremes – to the diagonal forecourt and both straight mid- and back court. Cross-court lifts and drive returns to your opponents' straight drops and smashes can be positively suicidal as these must pass through the racket areas of well positioned attackers. The answer is not that you must *not* play cross-court shots but that you must do so 'with discretion'.

STRIKING DOWN THE MIDDLE OF THE COURT

Essentially your opponents' defensive formation, designed to allow them to defend against shots directed to their fore-, mid- and back courts, has one flaw. Shots hit between the defenders can create uncertainty about which one should respond. From time to time, therefore, direct drops, smashes and clears (preferably flat and

fast) down the middle may provoke loose returns if not outright winners.

Mixed Doubles

All the considerations so far outlined for singles and level doubles play can be applied to mixed doubles. Some will have to be adapted to meet the specific mixed doubles needs, for example, that the lady will most often be the front player. We will first consider the possible exceptions and/or adaptions to statements made then add further considerations.

COURT POSITIONS

'The player nearest to the net dictates court positions when changing from the attack to defensive formation and subsequent court formation changes'. This statement stands except that the lady will not withdraw totally from the forward position. Her movements are only far enough back to allow a better opportunity to protect her side against drops and smashes. Only in exceptional, and preferably very well-considered and well-rehearsed circumstances will she move back far enough to deal with clears from the back court.

FORWARD PLAYER

'The forward player should never be astride the service line T-junction' and must 'base behind the front service line'. Both statements stand, but when the shuttle has been lifted high to the back of the opponent's court the lady should, most often, be basing on that side of the centre line which is diagonally opposite the opponent next about to hit the shuttle, whether man or lady. The principle is called 'cross-courting the striker'. In this situation the lady would expect assistance from her partner should the next shot be a straight drop!

ONE PLAYER ATTACKING

'Allowing only one player to maintain an attacking rally can pay dividends'. The well-organised mixed doubles pair can incorporate this principle to great effect. The man can fiercely attack the low serve and stay forward to hit hard any block returns. The man can hit a straight smash and then deal severely with the straight block return designed to catch out his partner. Note that in both instances the man must not treat any of the shots timidly, leaving his partner to try to cope with returns directed back to the net, nor must he play shots which leave both members of the partnership stranded in the forecourt.

As mentioned in an earlier chapter this principle also applies to the lady when responding to flick or drive serves. She plays shots positively designed to allow her to move quickly forward in anticipation of the probable replies. The lady must have her partner's co-operation to allow her, on occasions, to take on the man who constantly endeavours to pass her with drives. She must know that her partner will deal with cross-court shots so that she may pursue the 'one player attacking' role whole-heartedly.

NOT THE SLEEPER BUT THE HUNTER

Unfortunately the chances of the front player (the lady) becoming the 'sleeper' are greater in mixed than in level doubles as the men engage in hard-struck driving, clearing and smashing wars of attrition. More on this subject below. The lady can counter this by using the suggestions made for level doubles. Base behind the front service line but *not* on or over the T-junction. As the front player you can hit the shuttle to the opponent's floor sooner than your partner so *hunt* for the shuttle by being constantly up on the toes. The alternative is to become the barely contributing, often totally frustrated, sleeper!

At the risk of being repetitive you are reminded that all of the other considerations, both singles and doubles, could have some validity and should be included in your mixed doubles strategy planning. Further specific considerations are as follows.

ATTACKING THE SERVES

All of the ladies' responses are covered in the original narrative – the following is directed at the man. The need to move into the mid- and back court areas quickly should not be an excuse for the man to compromise the manner in which he receives the opponent's serves. But there is the obvious danger of his becoming stranded at the net unless the partnership has well-rehearsed procedures for these situations. The man must take up a very forward receiving stance with the aim of making an outright winner of his return. His partner will assist this intention by taking up a position of readiness behind him but on the other side of, not astride, the centre line. The procedures are then as follows.

The man aims to produce an outright winner off the low serve but only with a straight shot. For blocked straight returns he stays at the net to kill the shuttle. For straight driven or lifted responses he moves quickly back. The lady moves quickly forwards and both have then assumed their preferred attacking formation.

If any of the responses to the man's attempted service kill are returned cross-court the lady should respond as follows. She moves quickly forwards to counter the block to the net. She cuts off hard drives then moves quickly forwards. She moves quickly back for lifted shots and responds with one of her flicked serve returns, then moves forwards. In all cases both players move swiftly into their preferred attacking formation.

To serves to the back of his receiving court the man simply leaps quickly back as the lady moves as quickly forward.

DEFENDING AGAINST SHOTS TO THE NET

Earlier statements regarding defensive formations, while offering logical solutions at that time, now leave the lady diagonally opposite the probably downwards-hitting striker and vulnerable to straight drops. In this situation the man must, in addition to covering the hard-hit straight shots and cross-court clears, be prepared to assist. This he does by covering the straight drop to the extreme corner, that is into, or very close to, the tram-lines. Drops to any other part of the fore court will be taken by the lady. When the man is obliged to cover the shot to the net the partnership will adopt the formation and principles of reorganisation outlined under Attacking the Serves.

THE LADY SHOULD BE MATCH WINNER

Most of a doubles partnership's winning shots are played by the front player. This should also be the case in mixed doubles. All too often in mixed doubles the men are guilty of conducting a game of men's singles with limited interventions from the ladies. As the accepted formation for the mixed game is that of attack the back player must constantly endeavour to hit down. More often than not adopting this policy should provide a large number of opportunities for hitting down from the forecourt and for the lady to become the match winner. Of

course this will only happen if the lady is totally dedicated to the principle of the all-out attacking front player!

In conclusion remember that tactics are no more than logical solutions to situations actually encountered in games play. They need sensible consideration and, in doubles play, discussion between partners. By themselves tactics do not produce winners. They can only be applied totally successfully if you are physically fit and have sufficient racket and body skills developed as a result of practice.

Fig 112   Thomas Stuer-Lauridsen of Denmark playing an overhead back shot. Compare this with Steve Butler's hitting position illustrated in Fig 5. Both techniques are valid and require practice.

7
Practice

As a player's ability improves, so will the need to perfect his techniques of shot making and court movement. There are few opportunities within the games situation for practising as the need to compete successfully completely overrides all other considerations. Dedicated players will therefore de- vote periods to practise shot-making away from the pressure of competitive play.

SKILL ROUTINES

The following basic skill routines are designed to allow players to practise their shot making techniques and associated court movements by playing pre-determined shots in a set sequence. Possibilities are almost endless, ranging from simple 'one shot per player' through to complex 'five shots per player' routines. Because they are 'routines', i.e., both shots and movements are arranged in a pre-determined set sequence, players can concentrate their efforts on acquiring perfect form. Routines can be 'built' upon; when a simple routine has been mastered, additional shots and movements can be added to increase the demands on a player's abilities. Conversely, more complex routines can be 'broken down' into smaller, simpler elements. Regardless of the degree of complexity, for the dedicated player they all have the virtue of providing enjoyable working practices.

Space allows only a few examples to be considered, which are related to the simple practices suggested in Chapters 3 and 5. All of the routines illustrated have two common factors. Between each shot the player must recover to a 'bounce-base' in the mid-court. All of the shots are played down the sides of the court to ensure maximum court coverage between the 'base' and the shots. As with earlier simple practices, it may be necessary to reduce the demands of court movement initially as patterns of moving and hitting are grooved. Ultimately, full court coverage is necessary to enact game-like situations realistically.

Each illustration shows just one set of shots but there are two sides to each! Perform the routines as illustrated and/or described then change places with your partner. Each of you becomes player number 1 in turn. As the routines are as much about movement as hitting, recover to base after each shot, adopt the readiness position then make a preparatory bounce before travelling into the hitting position for the next shot.

All of the routines are played for a specific number of times or a set time. For example, each player could perform six sequences of a routine before changing roles with his partner. Alternatively the set routine is played as many times as possible in a set period of (say) 30 seconds.

Clear / Clear
(Fig 113)

1.1 Player 1 – high serve to backhand corner.
1.2 Player 2 – round the head forehand clear.
1.3 Player 1 – high overhead forehand clear.
1.4 Player 2 – round the head forehand clear. (The round the head forehand clear can be changed to backhand clear to provide another routine.)

Smash / Block Return / Net Return / High Lift
(Fig 114)

First version as illustrated:
1.1 Player 1 – round the head forehand smash.
1.2 Player 2 – forehand block return.
1.3 Player 1 – backhand net return.
1.4 Player 2 – forehand high lift.
Second version (not illustrated):
2.1 Player 1 – wide of head forehand smash.
2.2 Player 2 – backhand block return.
2.3 Player 1 – forehand net return.
2.4 Player 2 – backhand high lift.
(The round the head forehand smash can be changed to backhand smash to provide another routine.)

Drop / Net Return / Net Return / High Lift
(Fig 115)

Proceed exactly as above but substitute drops for smashes and net returns for the block returns. Do the same for backhand drops.

Clear / Drop / Net Return / High Lift
(Fig 116)

First version as illustrated:
1.1 Player 1 – wide of head forehand clear.
1.2 Player 2 – round the head forehand drop.
1.3 Player 1 – forehand net return.
1.4 Player 2 – backhand high lift.
Second version (not illustrated):
2.1 Player 1 – round the head forehand clear.
2.2 Player 2 – wide of head forehand drop.
2.3 Player 1 – backhand net return.
2.4 Player 2 – forehand high lift.
(The round the head shots can be changed to backhands to provide two further routines.)

Drop / Net Return / High Lift / Drop
(Fig 117)

1.1 Player 1 – wide of head forehand drop.
1.2 Player 2 – backhand net return.
1.3 Player 1 – forehand high lift.
1.4 Player 2 – round the head forehand drop.
(The round head forehand drop can be changed to backhand drop to provide another routine.)

Variations

As will be seen from the above, most, if not all, routines can be played in different ways. The examples show just two players on court but we could have up to four.

STRAIGHT WITH FOUR PLAYERS PER COURT
All shots are played 'straight' along one side of the court, usually between the tram-lines, to maximise travel from and recovery to base between shots by all of the players.

111

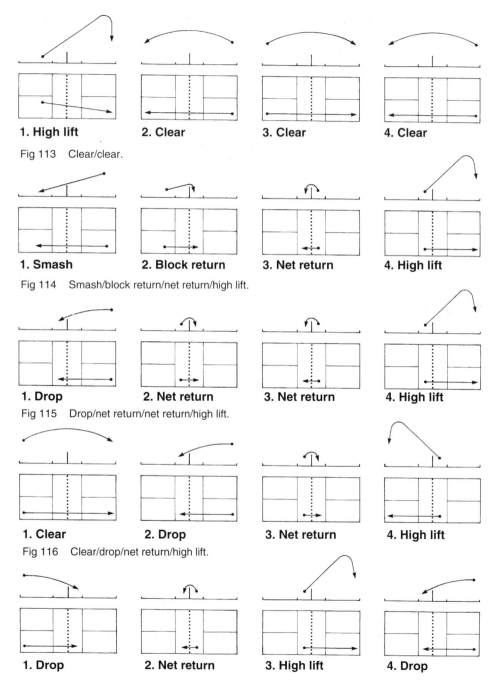

1. High lift **2. Clear** **3. Clear** **4. Clear**

Fig 113 Clear/clear.

1. Smash **2. Block return** **3. Net return** **4. High lift**

Fig 114 Smash/block return/net return/high lift.

1. Drop **2. Net return** **3. Net return** **4. High lift**

Fig 115 Drop/net return/net return/high lift.

1. Clear **2. Drop** **3. Net return** **4. High lift**

Fig 116 Clear/drop/net return/high lift.

1. Drop **2. Net return** **3. High lift** **4. Drop**

Fig 117 Drop/net return/high lift/drop.

CROSS-COURT WITH FOUR PLAYERS PER COURT

A straight routine is converted to cross-court by playing all of the shots through the diagonals of the court, i.e., from right to left and vice versa.

ONE AGAINST ONE

Routines are played by one player to the other all over a full singles court. You can dictate which shots are played or allow each player to decide which to use, e.g., from the backhand corner, round the head forehands or backhands.

ONE AGAINST TWO

One player, the 'worker', plays over a full singles court against two other players, the 'feeds', each of whom is responsible for his half of the court. The worker plays the routine first against one feed then switches to the second feed, plays the routine against him then switches back to the other and so on. Feeds are allowed to play their shots all over the full singles area – the worker must return his shots to the feed he is working against at the time.

OPTIONAL

This is most applicable to the one to one or one to two working situations. The predetermined shot sequence of shots is maintained, but each player has the option of playing his shots to any part of the available court area.

EITHER / OR

Ultimately this variation must be introduced to all of the routines with the objective of removing predictability and making them evermore competitive. The Drop/Drop routine (Fig 117) once mastered, is made far more demanding by allowing just one of the players to play shots in no particular order and introduce a further shot. The worker must observe the dictates of the routine by always playing a drop when the shuttle is played to the back of the court or a net return when the shuttle is played to the net. The other player is allowed to play either a drop, in which case the shuttle must be returned to the net, or a clear which must be returned as a drop to the net.

PRESSURISED

Again, this element is applicable to most, if not all, routines. Consider again our very basic Drop/Drop routine (Fig 117). Each player must now play all, or any, of the shots with additional pace, fast drops not slow, tight net shots not loose, taken at the top of the net not low down, lifts will have fast, flat trajectories not high and lofted. The total emphasis is on speed, with the player best able to keep up the pace becoming the winner.

TERMINATING

This element can be introduced into most routines – it is basically an extension of pressurising. In its simplest form it requires both players to endeavour to terminate a routine by attacking any of the shots within it at the earliest opportunity. Alternatively, only one of the shots may be selected, for example the net return of the Drop/Drop routine may be terminated with a net kill whenever possible. Otherwise it is to be lifted and the routine continued. Anticipating is not allowed, the net return can only be hit down following a leap lunge from the attacker's base.

SCORING

With 'Variations' the routines have become progressively more competitive, rather than co-operative. Now add further interest and even more competition by allowing points to be scored. The players score points when the other player is unable, for whatever reason, to maintain the rally dictated by the routine.

SUMMARY

The dedicated player must constantly spend time perfecting techniques outside the limiting environment of the usual club and match play situation. Those players with exceptional ability achieved this because they progressively spent more time training the body and practising their technical skills than in playing games.

Practising with the use of routines allows far more opportunities for hitting shuttles than exist in normal club play. Used correctly, this form of on-court practice ensures that techniques are perfected in their entirety, that is, with complete coverage of the court and, progressively, when under pressure.

It is not possible within this book to provide a comprehensive schedule of all the routines that can be used. Those shown give an idea of what is possible and cover all of the shots, allowing the reader to develop them further.

The illustrations are diagrammatic and do not attempt to show the variety of shots available, e.g., slices, changes of pace, different trajectories, and so on. Most importantly, they do not illustrate court movement to and from base. It is essential that these mainly diagonal movements are incorporated into all of the routines as applicable to the shots just played and to be played. You should not employ straight running between shots, other than where applicable, or perhaps when you are learning the routines.

8
Fitness Training

Players can become fitter as a result of playing badminton only. However, this would almost certainly be limited by their skill, for, to enter into long rallies, which are fitness building, they must have sufficient skills to maintain them. Unfortunately, without good physical condition they will be unable to employ their skills for long periods at a stretch.

Assuming that you had unlimited availability of courts and time, a well-planned, long-term, on-court training schedule would assist by balancing improving skills to ever greater physical demands. However, enhanced physical condition is much sooner achieved if on-court practices are complemented by an off-court programme of training. Remember the old adage: a player should get fit to play the game, not use the game to get fit!

ELEMENTS OF FITNESS

Research has shown that the physically fit person withstands fatigue for longer periods than the unfit; that the physically fit person has a stronger and more efficient heart; and that there is a relationship between good mental alertness, absence of nervous tension and physical fitness. For skilled players to become well-trained badminton athletes they need to develop both muscular and organic power in excess of the demands of long three-set matches. Skilled players will need to develop fast recovery rates both during a match and between matches, and for any other matches that follow. Therefore, the dedicated player must have a well thought out fitness programme.

The Six 'S' Factors and Rest

The aspiring badminton athlete should enter into an on-going fitness programme of both on-court and off-court training. This will seek to develop the six 'S' factors of Stamina, Strength, Suppleness, Speed, Skill and Sychology.

Stamina that is, cardio-respiratory endurance, is essential if you are to sustain intense activity throughout games. Good endurance is dependent upon the efficient working of the heart, lungs and circulation. It can be improved by regular, vigourous training which causes an increase in heart rate to well above double the resting pulse rate.

Strength refers to the capacity of muscles to exert force. In badminton, the ability to sustain short, very explosive bursts of power and speed is essential. Increased strength provides improved performance in jumping higher, lunging further, moving more dynamically.

115

Suppleness refers to the range of motion of the joints and the extensibility of the muscles. It determines the range that the limbs can move through and is an important factor in the avoidance of injury.

Speed is of two types: quickness of movement about the court and speed of executing a technique.

Skill is the ability to apply the right technique at the right time in the right place to achieve a desired outcome.

pSychology has a vital role to play in the player's preparation for competition. The programme also serves as a means of learning to combat stress and anxiety, of building inner confidence and developing a sense of dedication.

Finally **Rest** A training programme should be a controlled balance of stress and recovery. Obviously the body must have time to recover from the stress of training. High activity depletes energy stores, produces waste products – in general, breaks down the body. Rest allows the body to recover, replenishes its energy stores, removes waste products and allows the body to build again.

THE TRAINING PROGRAMME

Important Under no circumstances should you enter into any form of fitness training if you have a history of cardio-vascular and/or respiratory illnesses, are currently suffering from strained muscles or just recovering from an illness. If in doubt consult your medical practitioner for advice. Ultimately this programme becomes extremely strenuous.

Training Intensity Levels

There are five training intensity levels to be considered. These different levels are expressed as a percentage of your Maximum Heart Rate (MHR) determined as follows:

MHR = 220 less age less resting pulse rate multiplied by one of the five training intensities.

Training intensity levels are as follow:
level 1 – 70% – Over-distance, Power
level 2 – 75% – Endurance, Power, Speed
level 3 – 80% – Endurance, Power
level 4 – 90% – Interval, Speed
level 5 – 95% – Peak Speed

Below are three examples of MHR for various ages and resting pulse rates.

Level	1	2	3	4	5
Age 13 RPR60	163	170	178	192	200
Age 34 RPR40	142	150	157	171	179
Age 47 RPR65	141	146	151	162	168

It will be immediately obvious that to achieve a conditioning effect pulse rates have to be lifted above 140 for the majority and, for the young, can on occasions exceed 200.

Studies show that a very hard-fought rally of 40 seconds of more can take the pulse rate up to and beyond Level 5! By this stage the body is working anaerobically for a period. Training at peak speed serves to condition anaerobic capacity.

Off-Court Training Components

The programme has nine Training Components and is designed to cover twelve months – six months out-of-season preparation and six of competition. The schedule of components is shown below.

	O/dist't	Endu'e	Inter'l	Pow/Str
1	100-1			
2	72–1	28–5		
3	48–1	28–2		28–5
4	72–1	28–5		
5	36–1	18–2	18–3	28–5
6		36–2	36–3	28–5
7	50–-1	50–4		
8	12–2	60–5	28–5	
9	18–2	54–5	28–5	

EXPLANATIONS OF HEADINGS AND FIGURES FOLLOWING HYPHENS

Over-distance Leisurely cycle rides or long, slow, runs. Never conducted above Level 1.

Endurance Shorter, much harder, cycle rides or runs. Always conducted at Level 2.

Interval Repeated work efforts of short duration and high intensity. Conducted at Levels 3, 4 and 5.

Power A number of high-repetition, low resistance strength exercises. Can rise to Level 5.

EXPLANATIONS OF PERCENTAGES

The first figure in each column indicates the percentage share of the different elements in each of the Training Components. For example, Component 1 is totally Over-distance at Level 1. Training Component 2 is divided 72 per cent (of time) to Over-distance at Level 1 and the rest to Strength Training, parts of which require Level 5 effort. Components are divided into four bands to cater for different starting fitness levels, age or time available or a combination of all of these. The percentages given as examples are based on Band 4 working times. Over-distance, Endurance and Interval can be performed for as few as 7 minutes to as many as 60 minutes, Power exercises from 18 minutes to as much as 24 minutes. Different weights, applicable to certain of the exercises, are applied to different bands.

Read the later paragraphs on use of the programme before deciding upon your starting point!

OFF-COURT TRAINING COMPONENTS

Particularly note that all these dictate the need for an exercise cycle. It will be virtually impossible to replicate the sustained efforts required for the periods indicated in any other way. An exercise cycle is also less injurious to the limbs and joints than any other manner of training. Determine your five intensity levels – the resting pulse rate should be checked over a number of days, probably very early or late in the day, i.e., when you are positively resting! Check the working pulse rate from time to time while exercising to ensure you are achieving the correct rates. The most easily found pulses are on the sides of the throat.

1 – Over-distance only
a) Cycling at 20km/h against a resistance which first achieves and then maintains Level 1 intensity throughout the entire period indicated in the band below.
Band 1: 30 minutes; Band 2: 40 minutes; Band 3: 50 minute;s Band 4: 60 minutes.

2 – Over-distance / Strength
a) Cycling at 20km/h against a resistance which first achieves and then maintains Level 1 intensity throughout the entire period indicated in the band below.

Band 1: 30 minutes; Band 2: 40 minutes; Band 3: 50 minutes; Band 4: 60 minutes.
b) Complete the Strength exercises for the periods indicated on the schedule under Bands 1, 2, 3 or 4.

3 – Over-distance / Endurance / Strength

a) Cycling at 20km/h against a resistance which first achieves and then maintains Level 1 intensity throughout the entire period indicated in the band below.
Band 1: 20 minutes; Band 2: 27 minutes; Band 3: 33 minutes; Band 4: 40 minutes.
b) Cycling at 20km/h against a resistance which first achieves and then maintains Level 2 intensity throughout the entire period indicated in the band below.
Band 1: 10 minutes; Band 2: 13 minutes; Band 3: 17 minutes; Band 4: 20 minutes.
c) Complete the Strength exercises for the periods indicated on the schedule under Bands 1, 2, 3 or 4.

4 – Over-distance / Interval / Strength

a) Cycling at 20km/h against a resistance which first achieves and then maintains Level 1 intensity throughout the entire period indicated in the band below.
Band 1: 23 minutes; Band 2: 30 minutes; Band 3: 37 minutes; Band 4: 45 minutes.
b) Cycling at 20km/h against a resistance which first achieves and then maintains Level 3 intensity throughout the entire period indicated in the band below.
Band 1: 7 minutes; Band 2: 10 minutes; Band 3: 13 minutes; Band 4: 15 minutes.
c) Complete the Strength exercises for the periods indicated on the schedule under Bands 1, 2, 3 or 4.

5 – Overdistance / Endurance / Interval / Strength

a) Cycling at 20km/h against a resistance which first achieves and then maintains Level 1 intensity throughout the entire period indicated in the band below.
Band 1: 15 minutes; Band 2: 20 minutes; Band 3: 25 minutes; Band 4: 30 minutes.
b) Cycling at 20km/h against a resistance which first achieves and then maintains Level 2 intensity throughout the entire period indicated in the band below.
Band 1: 8 minutes; Band 2: 10 minutes; Band 3: 12 minutes; Band 4: 15 minutes.
c) Cycling at 20km/h against a resistance which achieves Level 3 intensity; sprint for 55 secs then slow cycle for 30 seconds then sprint for 55 seconds and so on for the total time indicated in the band below.
Band 1: 7 minutes; Band 2: 10 minutes; Band 3: 13 minutes; Band 4: 15 minutes.
d) Complete the Strength Exercises for the periods indicated on the schedule under Bands 1, 2, 3 or 4.

6 – Endurance / Interval / Strength

a) Cycling at 20km/h against a resistance which first achieves and then maintains Level 2 intensity throughout the entire period indicated in the band below.
Band 1: 15 minutes; Band 2: 20 minutes; Band 3: 25 minutes; Band 4: 40 minutes.
b) Cycle against a resistance which allows Level 4 intensity to be achieved after 20 seconds, then maintain for a further 25 seconds. 'Rest' by reducing resistance and cycling very slowly for 45 seconds. Repeat Accelerate to Level 4 in 20 seconds, hold for 25 seconds, reduce resistance and 'rest' for 45 seconds. Do this for the total period indicated in the band below.
Band 1: 15 minutes; Band 2: 20 minutes; Band 3: 25 minutes; Band 4: 30 minutes.
c) Complete the Strength exercises for the periods indicated on the schedule under Bands 1, 2, 3 or 4.

7 – Over-distance / Interval

a) Cycling at 20km/h against a resistance which first achieves and then maintains Level 2 intensity throughout the entire period indicated in the band below.

Band 1: 15 minutes; Band 2: 20 minutes; Band 3: 25 minutes; Band 4: 30 minutes.

b) Cycle against a resistance which allows Level 4 intensity to be achieved after 20 seconds, then maintain for a further 25 seconds. 'Rest' by reducing resistance and cycling very slowly for 45 seconds. Repeat. Accelerate to Level 4 in 20 seconds, hold for 25 seconds, reduce resistance and 'rest' for 45 seconds. Do this for the total period indicated in the band below.

Band 1: 15 minutes; Band 2: 20 minutes; Band 3: 25 minutes; Band 4: 30 minutes.

8 – Endurance / Interval / Strength

a) Cycling at 20km/h against a resistance which first achieves and then maintains Level 2 intensity throughout the entire period indicated in the band below.

Band 1: 5 minutes; Band 2: 7 minutes; Band 3: 9 minutes; Band 4: 10 minutes.

b) Cycle against a resistance which allows Level 5 intensity to be achieved after 20 seconds, then hold for a further 25 seconds. 'Rest' by reducing resistance and cycling very slowly for 45 seconds. Repeat. Accelerate to Level 5 in 20 seconds, hold for 25 seconds, reduce resistance and 'rest' for 45 seconds for the total period indicated in the band below.

Band 1: 15 minutes; Band 2: 20 minutes; Band 3: 25 minutes; Band 4: 30 minutes.

c) Complete the Strength exercises for the periods indicated on the schedule under Bands 1, 2, 3 or 4.

9 – Endurance / Interval / Strength

a) Cycling at 20km/h against a resistance

which first achieves and then maintains Level 2 intensity throughout the entire period indicated in the band below.

Band 1: 7 minutes; Band 2: 10 minutes; Band 3: 12 minutes; Band 4: 15 minutes.

b) Cycle against a resistance which allows Level 5 intensity to be achieved after 20 seconds, then hold for a further 25 seconds. 'Rest' for varying intervals after each sprint as follows.

Sprint 45 seconds cycle slowly 45 seconds
Sprint 45 seconds cycle slowly 30 seconds
Sprint 45 seconds cycle slowly 15 seconds
Sprint 45 seconds cycle slowly 15 seconds
Sprint 45 seconds cycle slowly 30 seconds
Sprint 45 seconds cycle slowly 45 seconds

Do this for the total number of minutes indicated in the band below.

Band 1: 23 minutes; Band 2: 30 minutes; Band 3: 38 minutes; Band 4: 45 minutes.

c) Complete the Strength exercises for the periods indicated on the schedule under Bands 1, 2, 3 or 4.

THE STRENGTH EXERCISES

All of these are illustrated below. The sets of numbers on the right-hand side of the following table are the number of seconds that the exercises are performed for each band. Regardless of band there is a common rest period of 20 seconds be-tween each exercise. Note that the last six exercises involve weights (be inventive, use a can of beans or whatever equates in weight) which vary for each ability band.

	Band			
	1	2	3	4
Warm-up and stretch				
Ordinary jumps	30	45	45	60
Racket Throwing – RH	45	60	60	60
Jumps and Lunges	30	45	60	60

119

Racket Throwing – RH	45	60	60	60
Tuck Jumps	30	45	60	60
Racket Net Tapping – LH	45	60	60	60
Racket Net Tapping – RH	45	60	60	60
Straight Sit-ups	30	30	45	60
Racket Block Tapping RH	45	60	60	60
Twist Sit-ups	30	30	45	60
Laying Straight Leg Lifts –RL	45	60	60	60
Laying Straight Leg Lifts – LL	45	60	60	60
Seated Lower Leg Lifts – RL	45	60	60	60
Seated Lower Leg Lifts – LL	45	60	60	60
Seated Upper Leg Lifts – RL	45	60	60	60
Seated Upper Leg Lifts – LL	45	60	60	60

Warm-down and Stretch

Weight to be worn (kilos)	1	1	2	3

Table of times (minutes) for Training Components

No.	B1	B2	B3	B4
1	30	40	50	60
2	42	62	73	84
3	42	62	73	84
4	42	62	73	84
5	42	62	73	84
6	42	62	73	84
7	30	40	50	60
8	32	49	57	64
9	30	40	50	60
Power	19	22	23	24

A MODEL PROGRAMME

The first consideration is the amount of time you are prepared to devote to a fitness programme. It must include on-court practices which, if conducted correctly, also have the same training components of Over-distance, Endurance, Interval and Power within them. And Rest periods must not be forgotten.

Authorities on the subject suggest that training volumes, expressed in hours per week, should/could vary from 3.85 for the beginner to 23 for world-class performers. It is interesting to note that even the world-class athlete does not train for more than four hours per day, assuming rest days are taken. The following model programme requires a maximum 8.9 hours per week if working at Band 4 levels.

The model programme assumes two on-court sessions each of two hours duration, which, with one day for rest and rehabilitation, leaves four others for off-court training and/or, in the season, competition. Training, both on and off court, is divided into three parts set against the fifty-two weeks of the year as follows:

1. Base (core)	MHR Levels 1, 2	56%
2. Intensity	MHR Levels 3, 4	14%
3. Peak	MHR 5	30%

In the model programme these percentages convert to Band 4 working times as below.

1. Base (core)	MHR Levels 1,2	228 hrs
2. Intensity	MHR Levels 3,4	55 hrs
3. Peak	MHR 5	122 hrs

From all of the above it should now be possible to prepare a twelve-month programme suited to individual needs, time available and ambition. There are three parts to the twelve-month programme as below.

Base/Intensity	22 weeks
Intensity/Peak	6 weeks
Peak/Competition	24 weeks

It will be seen that 'core' training starts 28 weeks before the programmed first competition. For the really dedicated performer consideration, preparation and implementation of a sensible, realisable programme is an essential annual task. See the model programme tables on page 122.

WHERE SHOULD YOU START?

Firstly, have you determined that you are fit for the task? Do not enter into a fitness training programme without a few, but very important, checks on your physical condition. Have a word with your doctor on the subject.

There are four bands of off-court training activity. They cater for all levels of ability, desire, dedication, age, commitment, and so on. Those under sixteen years old or over forty will sensibly settle for working with a low, rather than high, band of off-court training activity. If you are already a dedicated adult player practising regularly and engaging in club, league and (possibly) county matches as well as a programme of tournaments then you will require nothing less than Band 4. Suggestions are as follows.

The junior, under fouteen years of age, equivalent of the above dedicated player should have the same on-court (OC) training regime, of two two-hour on-court sessions per week, but work at Band 1 levels off-court. This suggestion is subject to assessment and consideration of parents and/or coach. Each year the player moves up one band to realise Band 4 by the age of seventeen or eighteen.

An adult beginner with a desire to match fitness levels to the ever-increasing demands arising from progressively improving skills, while not necessarily spending four hours on court, starts with Band 1 .

The adult player engaging in club play should be on at least Band 2. That same player once selected to play in league matches should then move to Band 3. Ultimately, if fitness, skills and dedication allow him to achieve county team selection, Band 4 will be an essential minimum.

Above all remember that the objective is to get fit to play the game. The six 'S' factors of the fitness programme relate to both off-court and on-court training. The objective of the overall training programme is to become a highly skilled and fit player of the game. Do not spend too much time on off-court training at the expense of your on-court skills practices; equally remember the earlier quoted adage: a player should get fit to play the game, not use the game to get fit. Achieve a sensible balance. Good levels of fitness should give you a feeling of well-being and allow you to work comfortably when practising rather than under pressure. In the competitive situation ensure that a lack of physical fitness is *not* the determining factor in the ultimate result.

Model for annual programme

Weekly Schedule of Components
OC = On-Court Cp = Competition R = Rest

	M	T	W	T	F	S	S
1	2	OC	1	OC	2	1	R
2	2	OC	1	OC	2	1	R
3	2	OC	1	OC	2	1	R
4	2	OC	1	OC	2	1	R
5	2	OC	1	OC	2	1	R
6	2	OC	1	OC	2	1	R
7	2	OC	1	OC	2	1	R
8	2	OC	1	OC	2	1	R
9	2	OC	1	OC	2	1	R
10	2	OC	1	OC	2	1	R
11	2	OC	1	OC	2	1	R
12	2	OC	1	OC	2	1	R
13	3	OC	1	OC	3	1	R
14	3	OC	1	OC	3	1	R
15	3	OC	1	OC	3	1	R
16	3	OC	1	OC	3	1	R
17	3	OC	1	OC	5	1	R
18	3	OC	1	OC	5	1	R
19	3	OC	1	OC	5	1	R
20	3	OC	1	OC	5	1	R
21	6	OC	8	OC	7	8	R
22	6	OC	8	OC	7	8	R
23	6	OC	8	OC	7	8	R
24	6	OC	8	OC	7	8	R
25	9	OC	1	OC	9	1	R
26	9	OC	1	OC	9	1	R
27	9	OC	1	OC	9	1	R
28	9	OC	1	OC	9	1	R
29	1	OC	2	OC	Cp	Cp	R
30	1	OC	2	OC	Cp	Cp	R
31	1	OC	2	OC	Cp	Cp	R
32	1	OC	2	OC	Cp	Cp	R
33	1	OC	2	OC	Cp	Cp	R
34	1	OC	2	OC	Cp	Cp	R
35	1	OC	2	OC	Cp	Cp	R
36	1	OC	2	OC	Cp	Cp	R
37	1	OC	2	OC	Cp	Cp	R
38	1	OC	2	OC	Cp	Cp	R
39	1	OC	2	OC	Cp	Cp	R
40	1	OC	2	OC	Cp	Cp	R
41	1	OC	2	OC	Cp	Cp	R
42	1	OC	2	OC	Cp	Cp	R
43	1	OC	2	OC	Cp	Cp	R
44	1	OC	2	OC	Cp	Cp	R
45	1	OC	2	OC	Cp	Cp	R
46	1	OC	2	OC	Cp	Cp	R
47	1	OC	2	OC	Cp	Cp	R
48	1	OC	2	OC	Cp	Cp	R
49	1	OC	2	OC	Cp	Cp	R
50	1	OC	2	OC	Cp	Cp	R
51	1	OC	2	OC	Cp	Cp	R
52	1	OC	2	OC	Cp	Cp	R

Hours per week to each Intensity Level

(Band 4 working)

	1	2	3	4	5	Total
1	7.33	–	–	0.73	0.73	8.79
2	7.33	–	–	0.73	0.73	8.79
3	7.33	–	–	0.73	0.73	8.79
4	7.33	–	–	0.73	0.73	8.79
5	7.33	–	–	0.73	0.73	8.79
6	7.33	–	–	0.73	0.73	8.79
7	7.33	–	–	0.73	0.73	8.79
8	7.33	–	–	0.73	0.73	8.79
9	7.33	–	–	0.73	0.73	8.79
10	7.33	–	–	0.73	0.73	8.79
11	7.33	–	–	0.73	0.73	8.79
12	7.33	–	–	0.73	0.73	8.79
13	6.12	1.22	–	0.73	0.73	8.80
14	6.12	1.22	–	0.73	0.73	8.80
15	6.12	1.22	–	0.73	0.73	8.80
16	6.12	1.22	–	0.73	0.73	8.80
17	6.00	1.10	0.47	0.43	0.67	8.67
18	6.00	1.10	0.47	0.43	0.67	8.67
19	6.00	1.10	0.47	0.43	0.67	8.67
20	6.00	1.10	0.47	0.43	0.67	8.67
21	–	2.90	–	2.70	2.70	8.30
22	–	2.90	–	2.70	2.70	8.30
23	–	2.90	–	2.70	2.70	8.30
24	–	2.90	–	2.70	2.70	8.30
25	2.00	0.60	–	–	6.30	8.90
26	2.00	0.60	–	–	6.30	8.90
27	2.00	0.60	–	–	6.30	8.90
28	2.00	0.60	–	–	6.30	8.90
29	2.00	–	1.00	0.20	3.00	6.40
30	2.00	–	1.00	0.20	3.00	6.40
31	2.00	–	1.00	0.20	3.00	6.40
32	2.00	0.60	1.00	0.20	3.00	6.40
33	2.00	0.60	1.00	0.20	3.00	6.40
34	2.00	0.60	1.00	0.20	3.00	6.40
35	2.00	0.60	1.00	0.20	3.00	6.40
36	2.00	0.60	1.00	0.20	3.00	6.40
37	2.00	0.60	1.00	0.20	3.00	6.40
38	2.00	0.60	1.00	0.20	3.00	6.40
39	2.00	0.60	1.00	0.20	3.00	6.40
40	2.00	0.60	1.00	0.20	3.00	6.40
41	2.00	0.60	1.00	0.20	3.00	6.40
42	2.00	0.60	1.00	0.20	3.00	6.40
43	2.00	0.60	1.00	0.20	3.00	6.40
44	2.00	0.60	1.00	0.20	3.00	6.40
45	2.00	0.60	1.00	0.20	3.00	6.40
46	2.00	0.60	1.00	0.20	3.00	6.40
47	2.00	0.60	1.00	0.20	3.00	6.40
48	2.00	0.60	100	0.20	3.00	6.40
49	2.00	0.60	1.00	0.20	3.00	6.40
50	2.00	0.60	1.00	0.20	3.00	6.40
51	200	0.60	1.00	0.20	3.00	6.40
52	2.00	0.60	1.00	0.20	3.00	6.40

STRENGTH EXERCISES

Warm up and stretch before starting. With each exercise, repeat it as often as possible in the time dictated by your band level, then rest for 20 seconds.

Ordinary jumps (Fig 118) Bounce on the toes, slightly flex knees then leap upwards, ex-tending hands to maximum height. Land lightly on toes and slightly flexed knees. Bounce, then leap again. Reach maximum height with each jump.

Squash racket throwing (Fig 119) Hold in right hand, upper arm close by side of head – racket head on chest. Quickly throw upper arm, then hand, to maximum height – a backhand clear! Allow racket to fall down over the back to touch the shoulder blade. Quickly throw upper arm, then hand, to maximum height – a forehand clear! Repeat as often as possible in the time dictated by your band level. Now rest for 20 seconds.

Jumps and lunges (Fig 120) Bounce on the toes, slightly flex knees then leap upwards extending hands to maximum height. Land lightly on toes and slightly flexed knees, bounce again then leap lunge to 'shadow' forehand net shot. Recover, leap upwards, bounce, leap lunge to "shadow" backhand net shot.

Squash racket throwing (Fig 121) Hold in left hand, upper arm close by side of head – racket head on chest. Quickly throw upper arm, then hand, to maximum height – a backhand clear! Allow racket to fall down over the back to touch the shoulder blade. Quickly throw upper arm then hand to maximum height – a forehand clear!

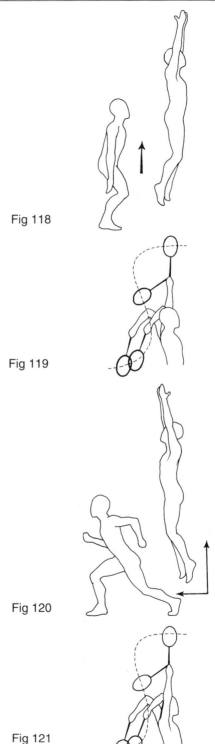

Fig 118

Fig 119

Fig 120

Fig 121

Tuck jumps (Fig 122) Bounce on the toes, slightly flex knees then leap upwards to maximum height. Keep hands down but tuck knees into chest. Land lightly on toes and slightly flexed knees. Bounce, then leap again. Try to reach maximum height with each jump.

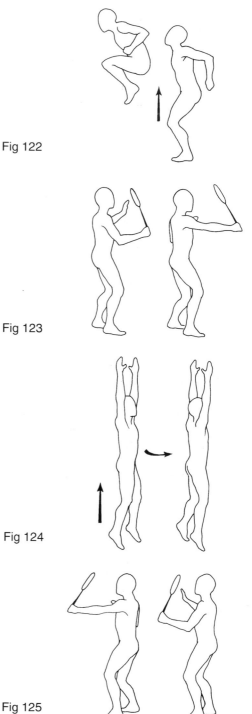

Fig 122

Squash racket net tapping (Fig 123) Stand square to an imaginary net with racket in right hand. Racket head above hand in 'pan-handle' grip. 'Net Tap' by rapidly extending hand quickly forward keeping racket vertical, first directly in front, then to the right, then (with a quick change to the backhand grip) to the left.

Fig 123

Jump turns (Fig 124) With your left shoulder towards imagined net, bounce on toes, slightly flex knees, then leap upwards turning body in mid-air to land with right shoulder to net. Land lightly with slightly flexed knees, bounce, leap back in opposite direction to starting point. Repeat as often as possible in time dictated by your band level. Now rest for 20 seconds.

Fig 124

Squash racket net tapping (Fig 125) Stand square to an imaginary net with racket in left hand, racket head above hand in 'pan-handle' grip. 'Net Tap' by rapidly extending hand quickly forward keeping racket vertical, first directly in front, then to the right, then (with a quick change to the backhand grip) to the left.

Fig 125

Straight sit-ups (Fig 126) Move to pre-pared work-station. Sit down in front of this and put feet over. Ensure bottom is cush-ioned, knees are comfortably bent and arms are folded. Perform good quality sit-ups with both elbows reaching out to both knees.

Fig 126

Squash racket blocking (Fig 127) Stand square to an imaginary net in 'receiving smash' stance, racket in right hand with head below hand in backhand grip. Tap by rapidly extending hand quickly forward keeping racket vertical, first directly off the front of the body, then to the left of the body, then (with a quick change to fore-hand grip) to the right. Repeat as often as possible in the time dictated by your band level. Now rest for 20 seconds.

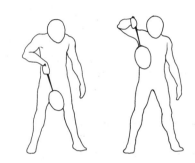

Fig 127

Twist sit-ups (Fig 128) Move to prepared 'work-station'. Sit down in front of this and put feet over. Ensure bottom is cushioned, knees are comfortably bent and arms are folded. Perform good quality sit-ups with with alternate twists: first right elbow to left knee, then left elbow to right knee.

Fig 128

Squash racket blocking (Fig 129) Stand square to an imaginary net in 'receiving smash' stance, racket in left hand with head below hand in backhand grip. Tap by rapidly extending hand quickly forward keeping racket vertical, first directly off the front of the body, then to the right of the body, then (with a quick change to fore-hand grip) to the left.

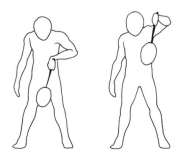

Fig 129

Reclining straight leg lefts (Fig 130) Lie on back (cushion under small of back) with weight as dictacted by your band level on right ankle. Keeping the leg straight throughout lift to 45 degrees. Lower to floor. Lift again and lower.

Fig 130

Reclining straight leg lifts (Fig 130) Lie on back (cushion under small of back) with weight as dictacted by your band level on left ankle. Keeping the leg straight through-out lift to 45 degrees. Lower to floor. Lift again and lower.

15 Seated lower leg lifts (Fig 131) Sit on a padded seat with weight as dictated by your band level on right ankle. Lift foot to just above the horizontal then lower. Avoid twisting the knee by ensuring that the foot stays in line with your thigh throughout the exercise.

Seated lower leg lifts (Fig 131) Sit on a padded seat with weight as dictated by your band level on left ankle. Lift foot to just above the horizontal then lower. Avoid twisting the knee by ensuring that the foot stays in line with your thigh throughout the exercise.

Fig 131

Now warm down and stretch.

Index